EXPERIENCING
GRIEF

H. NORMAN WRIGHT

BROADMAN
&HOLMAN
PUBLISHERS

NASHVILLE, TENNESSEE

0-8054-3092-X

Published by Broadman & Holman Publishers,
Nashville, Tennessee

Dewey Decimal Classification: 152.4
Subject Heading: GRIEF \ BEREAVEMENT \ JOY AND
SORROW

All Scripture quotations, unless otherwise indicated, are from
the Holy Bible, New International Version, copyright © 1973,
1978, 1984 by International Bible Society. Other versions
include: NCV, New Century Version, © 1987, 1988, 1991 by
Word Publishing, Dallas, Texas, 75039, used by permission;
TLB, The Living Bible, copyright © Tyndale House Publishers,
Wheaton, Ill., 1971, used by permission; *The Message*, the New
Testament in Contemporary English, ©1993 by Eugene H.
Peterson, published by NavPress, Colorado Springs, Colo.;
AMP, The Amplified Bible, Old Testament copyright © 1962,
1964 by Zondervan Publishing House, used by permission,
and the New Testament © The Lockman Foundation 1954,
1958, 1987, used by permission; NASB, the New American
Standard Bible, © the Lockman Foundation, 1960, 1962, 1963,
1968, 1971, 1972, 1973, 1975, 1977; used by permission;
N.L.T., The New Living Translation—published by the Christian
Literature International, Canby, Oregon, and is used by permission; and KJV, King James Version.

1 2 3 4 5 6 7 8 9 10 08 07 06 05 04

Contents

Preface

Iwill never forget the words, "In the next hour your son's heart and lungs will fail." There was such a sense of loss, helplessness, and finality. We had experienced a life of losses with him because he was disabled, but this was different. Throughout our lifetime we will experience the loss of friends and family members. Every loss brings pain and disruption of life. Death is no stranger to any of us, but the closer one is to you the greater the impact.

A common thread links us all together no matter who we are. It's called grief—the walk through the valley of shadows. It's a journey that is imposed upon us. It's not one of choice. We can fight it, struggle through it, or embrace it. Unfortunately, many don't understand it, which increases their level of discomfort.

My purpose in writing this book is to help you progress through this journey with a greater sense of comfort and hope. It may not make it easier, for grief is work—and sometimes very hard work.

I'm indebted to the hundreds of grieving people I've sat with over the years. It is their journey, their insights and wisdom and struggles that have taught me more about grief than my own experience.

If you're reading this book, you're probably somewhere on the path of grief. I hope this book helps to answer your questions, keep you on track when you tend to stumble, understand what to expect, and normalize what you are experiencing. If this occurs, then the crafting of this book has met its purpose.

Introduction

In a culture that doesn't like to acknowledge loss or talk about the impact, it's difficult to grieve. And when we add this silence to the fact that most of us have never been taught about the process and normalcy of grief, no wonder we struggle.

Perhaps you experienced what many have: you've been encouraged to have "lite" grief. "Get over it as soon as possible." "Isn't it time for you to move on with your life?" There are messages that increase the pain of grief.

If you are reading this book, you're probably experiencing grief and searching for some answers. Perhaps you sought support and assistance in this journey, but it's been difficult to discover others who can help rather than hinder. Others may have already tried to "fix you." Just remember, you don't need to be fixed. What could be needed is a greater understanding of the various faces of grief, what you can expect in the future, and what you can do to move forward.

This book was written out of a sense of need for everyone to understand the process and normalcy of grief. Many feel they're odd or different or even losing their senses. They believe, "I'm the only one to experience this." If you feel that way, you're not alone. It's just that many don't talk about their grief or can't tell you what to expect.

Let this book be your guide. Through twenty or so brief chapters, you will learn what grief is, what you can expect to experience, how to embrace your grief, and the steps to recovery. You can also realize you're not the only one to feel this way. My hope is that through the illustrations and information, you will discover that you are normal. Take your time. Read what you need. Go back and read again. Ask a friend to read aloud to you. You may not connect the first time you read a portion or remember it. It's all right. That's your grief. It does that to us. It overshadows our abilities and changes the way we see life. It's heavy. It weighs us down and deadens our senses. And it lasts far longer than we want. But learn from it. It's a great teacher. You and I will be different because of our grief. Your walk with God may also be different—even deeper, as it was with Job.

> My ears had heard of you before, but now my
> eyes have seen you. (Job 42:5 NCV)

As you reflect on the various Scriptures and allow the truth of the Word of God to be your companion, I pray that you will experience his comfort.

CHAPTER I

The Faces of Grief

The world is full of faces. Some familiar, some unfamiliar. Many are constant companions. They belong to those closest to us—a friend, a parent, a grandparent, a spouse, or a child. But one day a face is missing. Its presence is no longer there. There's an empty spot, but not for long. A new face emerges to take its place. It's unfamiliar and unfriendly. It's the face of grief.

Grief—what do you know about this experience? We use the word so easily. It's the state we're in when we've lost a loved one. It's an inward look. You've been called into the house of mourning. It's not a comfortable place. It's not where you want to reside, but for a time, longer than you wish, you will. Often it will hurt, confuse, upset, and frighten you. It's described as intense emotional suffering or even acute sorrow.

In grief the bottom falls out of your world; the solid footing you had yesterday is gone. It feels more like a floorboard tilting or soft pliable mud with each step you take. The stability of yesterday's emotions has given way to feelings that are so raw and fragile you think you are losing your mind. We feel alone with it, yet we're not for Jesus himself was there, "a man of sorrows, acquainted with bitterest grief" (Isa. 53:3 TLB).

Mourning is the second part of the experience. This is the process where grief is expressed. It's a natural, God-given process of recovery. It's his gift to us to help us get

3

through the pain. Everyone has grief, but mourning is a choice. You cannot make your grief better, make it go away, fix it, or just "get over it."

Before you take a journey into an unknown land, you usually consult a map. Grief is a journey that moves across unknown terrain that includes valleys and mountains, the arid desert with an occasional oasis. Most of us look at a map, and we begin a cross-country trip exploring new places. Most of us don't look at a map of the grief experience, so we end up questioning the experiences, "Are these feelings normal?" "Am I normal?" Each part of this journey can only be accomplished by moving through it. It's slow, one step at a time, and you'll hit bottom. And you're not always sure where you're going to end up, or where the journey ends.

Sometimes in your grief you may feel that you're on a crooked sidewalk, just being pushed along without being able to stop, look around, get your bearings, and decide whether this is the direction you want to go. Grief brings you into the world of the unknown.

THE WORD PICTURES OF GRIEF

There are many word pictures that others have created to describe the experience of grief. Often when we read these, we say, "Yes. That's exactly the way I feel. I thought I was the only one." You're not. This is normal grief.

A grieving father said:

> Grief is like a wave. It comes rolling in from a far-off place. I could no more push it back than if I were standing in the water at the beach. I could not fight the wave. It moved over me and under me and broke against me, but I could never stop it. It yielded to my presence and in so yielding arrived at its destination. It worked around me. The harder I fought it, the more exhausted I became. So it is with grief. If I tried to fight it, it would vanquish me. If I pushed

it down it would stick in my soul and emerge as something else: depression, bitterness, exhaustion. If I yielded to the waves and let it carry me, however, it would take me to a new place.[1]

And so it is with grief. It takes you to the tops of the waves, and then they break, and you struggle in the froth of emotion. It also brings memories. It will expose who we really are inside. Waves run out of energy. As they move closer to the shore, their power is spent, and they slowly bubble up to the edge of the sand. The more we stand and fight and rail against the waves, the more exhausted we become. It's an exercise in futility. The more you accept it, hold out your arms to it, and even embrace it, the more you will recover. We need to take a step that for many of us is difficult—yield. Yield to your grief. Let it do its work in your life and mourn.[2]

When you enter into grief, you enter into the valley of shadows. There is nothing heroic or noble about grief. It is painful. It is work. It is a lingering process. But it is necessary for all kinds of losses. It has been labeled everything from intense mental anguish to acute sorrow to deep remorse. As some have said, "It's a feeling of heaviness. I have this overwhelming oppressive weight which I can't shed."

A multitude of emotion is involved in the grief process—emotions that seem out of control and often appear in conflict with one another. With each loss comes bitterness, emptiness, apathy, love, anger, guilt, sadness, fear, self-pity, and helplessness. These feelings have been described in this way:

These feelings usher in the emotional freeze that covers solid ground with ice, making movement in any direction seem precarious and dangerous. Growth is hidden, progress seems blocked, and one bleakly speculates that just because the crocuses made it through the snow last year is no reason to believe they can do it again this year. It's not a pretty picture.[3]

We will talk about these feelings again.

Perhaps this description of land in the Dust Bowl in Oklahoma in the 1930s is descriptive of your life at this time:

> A day went by and the wind increased, steady, unbroken by gusts. The dust from the roads fluffed up and spread out and fell on the weeds beside the fields. . . . Little by little the sky was darkened by the mixing dust, and the wind felt over the earth, loosened the dust, and carried it away. The wind grew stronger. . . . The corn threshed in the wind and made a dry, rushing sound. The finest dust did not settle back to earth now, but disappeared into the darkening sky.
>
> The wind grew stronger, whisked under stones, carried up straws and old leaves, and even little clods, marking its course as it sailed across the fields. The air and the sky darkened and through them the sun shone redly, and there was a raw sting in the air. During the night the wind raced faster over the land, dug cunningly among the rootlets of corn, and the corn fought the wind with its weakened leaves until the roots were freed by the prying wind and then each stalk settled wearily sideways toward the earth and pointed the direction of the wind.
>
> The dawn came, but no day. In the gray sky a red sun appeared, a dim red circle gave a little light, like dusk; and as that day advanced, the dusk slipped back toward darkness, and the wind cried and whimpered over the fallen corn.
>
> Men and women huddled in their houses, and they tied handkerchiefs over their noses when they went out, and wore goggles to protect their eyes.

When the night came again it was a black night, for the stars could not pierce the dust to get down, and the window lights could not even spread beyond their own yards. Now the dust was evenly mixed with the air, an emulsion of dust and air. Houses were shut tight, and cloth wedged around doors and windows, but the dust came so thinly that it could not be seen in the air, and it settled like pollen on the chairs and tables, on the dishes.[4]

An upheaval not only alters the landscape but often deforests the landscape, leading to further devastation. The same thing can happen when tragedy strikes the small, forty-acre farm that is our life.

Steinbeck's description of the Dust Bowl is what the weather of the heart is sometimes like for someone who has endured a great loss. A steady wind blows over you, opposes you, oppresses you. The wind grows stronger, whisking away what little soil surrounds the few rootlets of spiritual life you have left. With the wind comes stinging reminders of how different your life is from everyone else's. Other people talk together, shop together, dine together, laugh together. And the taken-for-granted normalness of their lives stings your face so raw you can't bear it. Your bloodshot eyes burn from the wind-blown grit. Your tears wash away the grit, but not the burn.

You lie in bed at night, staring at the ceiling. Your thoughts are incoherent pieces of a puzzle you have grown weary of, yet can't get rid of. The headache won't go away. Or the guilt. Or the regret. You're out of tears, out of prayers. You've waited in silence, wept in silence, wondered in silence. You wonder if anyone is up there, beyond the ceiling, if

anyone was *ever* up there, or if it has all been just
so much pious talk and positive thinking, reinforced
by the peer pressure of your religious friends.

Outside the sky is darkened. The night is black.
Light from heaven, once as sparkling as a star-
studded sky, cannot pierce the airborne dust. What
little light you have within you doesn't spread very
far, either.

Through the night the wind continues. The night
is long and it seems the dawn will never come.
Finally the dawn comes, but no day. A gray sky
veils the sun. And God, who once seemed so radi-
ant, now seems a dim red circle that gives little
light.

Eventually the wind subsides, the dust settles,
and it is safe to go outside again. What then? How
do we reclaim the Dust Bowl that our life has
become? Where do we even start?[5]

Has this description been your experience? For many in
grief it has. Perhaps you are wanting to reclaim the Dust
Bowl of your life. The first step to accomplish this is understanding your grief now, in the future, and the fact that
what you are experiencing is normal.

CHAPTER 2
Pain and Denial

With any loss comes grief, and a companion of grief is pain. The pain of grief can be overwhelming. It's like a visitor who has overstayed his welcome. There will be days when you want this experience to be history. As you look around, you see the sun and billowing clouds. You wonder how it can shine like this while you have so much despair. How can life continue its steady progress in coming and going? How can flowers bloom and people laugh while your heart has broken? And as grief continues, the more you feel that things will never get better. But they will. Oh, they will.

We are not immune to pain, but we resist its intrusion. There are several ways we use to do this. Some fight the pain through denial. We say, "No, it isn't true" or attempt to live our lives as though nothing has happened. When you hear about the death, your first response is often, "No, that's not true. Tell me it isn't so! No" or, "You're mistaken." You're trying to absorb the news, and it takes time to filter through the shock. This is normal. You're trying to make sense of the nonsensical. But some continue this process, and that's what we call sensible. When asked how they are doing, their response is always, "I'm doing just fine," instead of honestly saying, "I am really hurting today." Denial can lead to even greater losses. The author of *A Grace Disguised* said of those who are unwilling to face their pain that "ultimately it diminishes the capacity of their souls to grow bigger in response to pain."[1]

Grieving is moving through several levels of denial. Each stage brings home the reality of the loss a bit deeper and more painfully. We accept it first in our heads, then in our feelings, and finally we adjust life's pattern to reflect the reality of what has occurred. There is a price to pay for prolonged denial. The energy that must be expended to keep denial operating drains us, and in time we can be damaged emotionally, delaying our recovery.

Denial is used to block out the unthinkable, but it brings with it the fear of the unknown since you are denying the reality of what happened. As denial lessens, the pain begins to settle in; and as it does, the fear of the unknown diminishes. Denial is a cushion. It may help for a while, but then it turns against you, and you may need to ask yourself, "Is this keeping me from moving forward in my life?"

When I was in high school in the 1950s the song "The Great Pretender" was released. Many in their grief take on this role as they attempt to act as though they are handling everything well. You may feel you have to keep up pretenses or your former schedule. You don't. And you don't need to be afraid of upsetting others. Right now your attention needs to be focused on your life.

Some deal with this pain by bargaining, indulging themselves, or venting anger. But all of these are ways of attempting to deflect the pain. Gerald Sittser said, "The pain of loss is unrelenting. It stalks and chases until it catches us. It is as persistent as wind on the prairies, as constant as cold in the Antarctic, as erosive as a spring flood. It will not be denied and there is no escape from it."[2] The psalmist knew this, "I weep with grief; my heart is heavy with sorrow" (Ps. 119:28 TLB).

Will the Scriptures help you with your pain? Yes and no. "The scriptures are not a medicine cabinet, filled with prescriptions to take the edge off of life. They are about a God who, during his most painful experience on earth, refused the wine mixed with myrrh that was offered him."[3]

It helps to deal with your pain a little bit at a time. Don't try to accomplish too much, for there will be times when you'll need to take a break from your grief.

CHAPTER 3

Grief Is So Disruptive

❧

Grieving is a disorderly process. You won't control it, nor can you schedule its expression.

Your grief will take the shape of a spiral figure rather than a linear one. Grief is not a straight line moving gradually up and toward a set point. You will move forward only to return to where you were. You think you've left behind that intense pain, and your relief is so refreshing, but you will rediscover the pain again and again. Was this your experience? When the loss of your loved one occurred, there was a flurry of activity as friends and other family members converged on your dwelling place. This was necessary. It brought comfort as friends shared, connected, and touched. These were gifts of food and hurts and tears and memories. The service where people gathered brought hope.

But in a few days there were no more services or family or friends. They went home, and you were left to face your new resident—grief. It's like cleaning away all the brush and weeds around your home, but everything gets overgrown again overnight. This is normal. You are normal.

Grief disrupts your mind and thinking ability. Confusion moves in and memory takes a vacation. If you experience short-term memory loss after the death, it's probably a result of the stress and anxiety you've experienced. Just as your leg can experience a cramp and not move, it's as though your mind has a memory cramp. Your mind is paralyzed and shuts down. The more you accept what is occurring, the sooner it will pass.

You may experience quite vividly your last interaction with the person who died. Some say the experience is so real it's as though you are actually there talking with them again. These experiences will pass. They're normal responses for what you've experienced.

You may find yourself easily distracted and perhaps disoriented even if you are normally a decisive person. You may discover now you're afraid to make choices. You end up feeling childlike. During the next few months, decisions will probably need to be made. It's not the best time of your life for these decisions because of your emotional wounds. But some can't be delayed. Financial, living, family members' decisions may not be avoidable at this time. But remember, major decisions during the first year will be flavored by intense emotions. Others will urge you to make a decision one way and someone else another. Take your time, don't be rushed, ask God to give you a clear mind and lead you to those who have your best interest at heart. When asked by others to decide, put in a delay. Say, "Thank you for your suggestion. I want to think and pray about this and I will let you know."[1]

You may find that your sense of time is distorted. Time goes too fast or too slow. Past and future collapse together. The future is hard to fathom. Some shut out both the past and the future, but we need both the memories and the hope. There is wisdom in this thought, "Reminiscing is intended to liberate you from emotional claims of the past in order to think hopefully about the future."[2]

When you grieve, your attention is not upon others. It's upon you. This too is normal. Your own intense feelings are probably all that you can bear at this time, and so for a brief time you may shut out the world. Sometimes this occurs because you're afraid that others will take away your feelings and memories, and that's all you have left.[3]

Whenever there is a loss, there will be grief. But some do not *grieve* or *mourn*. Some make a choice not to express all the feelings inside so their grief is accumulated. Saving it won't lessen its pain. It will only intensify it. Silence covers wounds before the cleansing has occurred. The result will be an emotional infection.

Some try to make others carry their burden. But grief can't be shared. Everyone has to carry it alone, his own burden, and in his own way.[4]

You may have said, "Where are they when I need them the most?" You'll probably say that about your friends.

The author of *Healing After Loss* said: "Now there are spaces in the mind, spaces in the days and night. Often, when we least expect it, the pain and the preoccupation come back and back—sometimes like the tolling crash of an ocean wave, sometimes like the slow ooze after a piece of driftwood is lifted and water and sand rise to claim their own once more."[5]

And so, during this loss you may incur yet another loss—your friends. You may have expected some to be by your side, but they never showed up; or if they did, they either weren't much help or they didn't return. Some won't know what to say since most have never been instructed on how to help others at a time such as this. Or perhaps they're dealing with some of their own grief. It may help to let them know that you would just like them to call you frequently, listen, help with a few tasks, or pray with you. (See the Appendix for resources you could recommend to them to help build their ability to help you and others.)

CHAPTER 4

The Nature of Grief

Grief is slow, and you need it to be like this even though you'll probably want to rush it along. It will take longer than you have patience for. Time seems to stand still especially at night. Don't let others rush you through this process. They're not experts, and you'll discover others will be uncomfortable with your grief. Let your grief do its healing work at its own slow pace. You need its slowness. Grief cannot be put on a fast track.

Don't compare your loss with others and think theirs is worse or more painful than your own. The worst loss is your own. It may have been gradual, or it could have been as sudden and traumatic as the planes crashing into the towers of New York. Some suffering builds gradually while for others it's instantaneous.

The worst loss is the one you are experiencing at this time. You may question that as you compare your loss with others you've heard about. You may have lost your grandparent, parent, brother or sister, or spouse. There is no other loss in our society that is so neglected as the death of a brother or sister. When you lose a sibling, you lose a person who was a part of your formative past, someone who has been in your life a long time. You may have lost a child; this is sometimes referred to as the ultimate bereavement. You're not supposed to outlive your child. Experiencing a miscarriage or stillbirth is still the death of a child. And to the expectant parents it is just as much a loss as losing a twenty-two-year-old son. But with certain types of deaths, you will not receive the same recognition or support as if you had lost a spouse, a child, or a parent. Miscarriages and stillbirths rarely receive the support they need. This is also true when you lose a friend in death. We will probably lose more friends in our lifetime than relatives. Harold Ivan Smith voiced a sentiment that most of us think but rarely say: "My friends, although dead, fill the bleachers of my memories."[1]

He also said: "Experiencing my friend's death has depleted my heart. My heart lies collapsed, like a party balloon the morning after the celebration. No one understands my grief. I guess that's what I get for taking friendship so seriously."[2]

Most of us have friends who are much closer than our relatives. Your loss now or in the past could have been a friend, but who encouraged you to grieve or supported you in your grief? Close friendships that last have been a great investment in trust, openness, vulnerability, affection, and warmth. When your friend dies, something has been ripped away. It's a great loss coupled with another hurt of your loss not being given the recognition and support it needs.

Everyone grieves and heals differently. Some want to be connected to people as much as possible. Others prefer to be left alone. Some prefer to take care of their own problems, while others want assistance. One prefers activity, while another prefers just the opposite. Others may attempt to fill your life with what you don't want. Even though it will take effort, you may need to let others know what you need as well as the best way for them to help you. When grief is your companion, you experience it in many ways. It permeates and changes your feelings, thoughts, and attitudes. It impacts you socially as you interact with others. You experience it physically as it affects your health and is expressed in physical symptoms.

You may be afraid you're not doing your grief "right." You will hear advice—usually unsolicited. You will also hear conflicting advice and "shoulds" and "shouldn'ts." There are many misguided notions about what "correct" or "healthy" grieving is about. You may experience most of what is discussed in this book, or you may not. Your grief experience is unique.

Grief encompasses a number of changes. It appears differently at various times, and it flits in and out of your life. It is a natural, normal, predictable, and expected reaction. It is not an abnormal response. In fact, just the opposite is true. The absence of grief does not have to be accepted or validated by others for you to experience and express grief.[3]

CHAPTER 5

Why Grief?

❧

Why grief? Why do we have to go through this experience? What is the purpose? Grief responses express basically three things:

1. Through grief you express your feelings about your loss. And you invite others to walk with you.

2. Through grief you express your protest at the loss as well as your desire to change what happened and have it not be true. This is a normal response.

3. Through grief you express the effects you have experienced from the devastating impact of the loss.[1] Through grief you may experience God in a new way that will change your life as Job said, "My ears had heard of you before. But now my eyes have seen you" (Job 42:5 NCV).

Along this difficult journey many experience what we call a "grief spasm." It's alarming since it's an intense upsurge of grief that happens suddenly and when least expected. It's disruptive and you feel out of control. Some describe it as continuing painful waves of grief. It won't take much to cause this to occur. Some refer to it as being ambushed by grief. When it happens, stop what you're doing and deal with your feelings until some level of calm is restored. The more you try to put these feelings on hold the more pain you will experience. You may feel these spasms are one of your worst times. See them, however, as normal. You may want to say to them, "I wish you weren't here, but I can handle you. And I will recover from this experience." Doing this can give you a greater sense of control.

You may be uncomfortable with your grief. So might others around you. They want you "normal" as soon as possible, or they want you to act as if you are. But you are not ready for it, and others should not be the ones to determine when you are ready. This is your loss, not theirs. No one should rob you of your grief. Some may attempt to do just that because they are uncomfortable. Many years ago someone commented, "When a person is born we celebrate; when they marry we jubilate; but when they die we act as if nothing has happened."[2] Something life changing has happened. It needs to be faced. Give others permission to be uncomfortable.

It's not unusual to hear those in grief say, "I resent my grief. I don't want it in my life. It's too painful. I want to do a grief bypass." Some have taken another step and written their grief a letter sharing their frustration, feelings, and complaints they have about their grief. If you do so, don't be concerned about your spelling or grammar or any editing. Just put down on paper all those thoughts and feelings. You may even want to describe what you've learned from your grief. Read your letter out loud either by yourself or to a trusted friend.

If you like, write another letter a week later. But this time have the letter written to *you* by your grief. After a week of reflection, what do you think your grief would say to you on how to deal with your grief? (For examples of such letters, see *Life after Loss* by Bob Diets, Fisher Books, 1988, 93–94.)

As much as grief hurts, there is another face to it. As one writer said, "There's a good reason for entering fully into one's sorrow. Once you have experienced the seriousness of your loss, you will be able to experience the wonder of being alive."[3]

Barbara Bumgartner's words might help you, "Grief is a statement—a statement that you loved someone."

When you experience the thoughts and feelings of grief, it moves you into unknown territory, but you need to walk through some wilderness.

And grief does have another side. Is it an easy journey? No. Is it a painless journey? No. Is it a controlled journey? No. Is the journey worth it? Yes. It will change you as a person and your perspective on life.

As you read this book, you will face grief head-on, learn from it, let it do its work. True, it's not always pleasant, nor are your days clear. During grief the day seems like night, often with a blanket of fog swishing about. The psalmist reflected this when he said, "When my spirit was over-whelmed within me" (Ps. 142:3 KJV). The words literally mean, "The muffling of my spirit." But as the grief begins to thaw, you will find the sun breaking through your gloom. The psalmist said, "Weeping may remain for a night, but rejoicing comes in the morning" (Ps. 30:5).

So as you live with the face of grief as your constant companion and wonder whether it's a life sentence, remember these words, "I tell you the truth, you will weep and mourn while the world rejoices. You will grieve, but your grief will turn to joy" (John 16:20).

CHAPTER 6

What Grief Does

Disruption, holes, confusion—the many faces of grief. The death of a loved one disrupts your entire life schedule. And the ensuing grief doesn't just impact one part of you. It's not something you select off a rack at a clothing store to cover a portion of your body. It comes from within and doesn't leave one particle of your life untouched. It's consuming. Your body changes. Food doesn't taste the same, nor will the fragrance of your favorite flower be as intense. The frequency of tears will cloud your vision. Some experience a tightness in their throat or chest, an empty feeling in their stomach, shortness of breath, or rapid heart rate. Eating and sleeping patterns won't be the same. Some sleep and sleep, while others wish that sleep would come. Sleep is either an easy escape, or it's elusive. You try to fall asleep, but your mind and emotions seem locked on your loss. You may wake up and stay awake for hours trying desperately to sleep. Dreams or nightmares occur. This disruption will decrease in time, but recovery is not a smooth, straightforward path; it's a forward-backward dance. Reflecting on the Word of God at times when sleep is difficult can comfort you.

> If I'm sleepless at midnight, I spend the hours in grateful reflection. (Ps. 63:6 *The Message*)

> When anxiety was great within me, your consolation brought joy to my soul. (Ps. 94:19)

Your mind is at work while you sleep. You probably wish it would shut down and rest so your body and emotions

could rest. But it's working the night shift, processing the
pain and loss in your life right now with memories both
accurate and bizarre. You'd just like some relief. But someone else is well aware of your dreams. There is another who
is working the night shift.

The psalmist described what occurs as you sleep, "He
who watches over you will not slumber; indeed, he who
watches over Israel will neither slumber nor sleep" (121:3–4).

Ron Mehl describes the work that is occurring:

> God is aware of your circumstances and moves
> among them.

> God is aware of your pain and monitors every
> second of it.

> God is aware of your emptiness and seeks to fill
> it in a manner beyond your dreams.

> God is aware of your wounds and scars and
> knows how to draw forth a healing deeper than you
> can imagine.

> Even when your situation seems out of control.

> Even when you feel alone and afraid.

> God works the night shift.[1]

Prior to the death of your loved one, your life was going
in a well-established direction. This has changed. You had
an identity. You could say who you were. This too has
changed. You are not exactly who you were. The person you
lost was part of your identity. You were someone's mother
or aunt or spouse or brother. You continue to be that person in your heart and memory, but there's a vacant place
where your loved one stood. And the loss of this person has
subtracted from you part of who you were. Eventually you
will take steps to move from the old to the new identity.[2]
This may be hard to grasp at this time, but someday . . .

You may also experience the "face in the crowd" syn-
drome. You think you saw the one you lost or heard their
voice or smelled their perfume or cologne. This can happen
at home or in public places as well. You might wake up at

night and swear you sensed their presence in the room or heard them call your name. We think we're going crazy and hesitate to share the experience with others for fear of what they will think. But this is more common than most realize and can last for as long as eighteen months.

It Wasn't You
I thought I saw you today
Standing there in the checkout line
Just out of reach.
I started to call your name
But I stopped.
My mind said it wasn't you,
Couldn't be you.
My heart said otherwise,
Vehemently.

I was embarrassed by the
Tears that sprang, unbidden
To wash away my
Disappointment.
I wrestled—like Jacob with the angel—
Until I had conquered, once more,
My grief.
The struggle left me feeling
Out of joint.

The world slipped away
    As I left the store.

There was only me
And my grief.
No you.
Never again a "you."
Finally, I grabbed my grief
By the neck, shouting,
"I will not let you go until you bless me!"
                                        —Lynn Brookside[3]

CHAPTER 7

Holes in Your Life

When you lose someone, holes are created in your life. There's a hole at the dinner table, in the seat next to you at church or the restaurant, on the other end of the phone, extra space in the house, less sound in the car. It takes weeks and months before you stop looking, searching, or reaching out in conversation as though the person were still there. Planning a typical routine or vacation now falls out of the routine category.

It's not just the loss of your loved one that is so painful. It's all the other losses that occur because of this one. The way you live your life, love, sleep, eat, work, and worship are all affected. Often the death of your loved one brings up not just grief for what you lost but also for what you never had and what you never will have. There is a loss of the present as well as the future. And this especially impacts your relationships. You may feel awkward around others for whom the one you lost was also a loved one. A death can put distance in some relationships or draw together and connect others in a greater intimacy than before. Death can be either a wedge or a source of confusion.

But like so many other areas of life, what occurs takes choices and courage on your part. Out of this painful chaos there will eventually be glimmers of something new. This is a thought to hold onto and file away since at this point in time this could be the furthest thought from your mind.

You will find that your loved one was the link to certain relationships, and now that the link is gone, some relationships may fade. Others may be too uncomfortable to continue the same kind of relationship. Some may become closer than ever before. You may feel that others are just continuing on without you and you're feeling left behind. Many in grief are thrown by the changes in relationships since no one forewarned them of this possibility.

You may be the one who wants to build or even end some of the relationships. Perhaps some were obligations held together by the other person. You may want to put this entire topic on hold until you're further along on your journey of grief.[1]

Your behavior changes. Many say, "I'm just not myself." That's true. You won't be for some time. You may find yourself phasing out when others are talking. Your mind drifts off since it's difficult to stay focused and attentive. You feel detached from people and activities even though they're an important part of your life. What is upsetting to many is how absent-minded you are. You may cry for "no apparent" reason. It's common to lose your sense of awareness of where you are in losses of both time and place. C. S. Lewis describes this apathy as the "laziness of grief." The feeling, "Oh, what's the use?" is a constant theme. Everything can seem to be such an effort. A man who lost his fiancé in an accident described this state: "I couldn't see one day ahead of me. I became a foot watcher, walking through airports or the grocery store staring at my feet, methodically moving through a misty world. One foot, then the other. . . . Some days, especially early on, it was the only act of faith I could muster."[2]

Your feelings could be more intense than you could imagine. They come and go with an overwhelming intensity, or they become entrenched as though encased in cement. Many describe them as recurring waves like the ocean. Scripture reflects what we experience.

Oh, my anguish, my anguish!
I writhe in pain.
Oh, the agony of my heart!
My heart pounds within me,
I cannot keep silent.
For I have heard the sound of the trumpet;
I have heard the battle cry. (Jer. 4:19)

Where do all your feelings come from in grief? Even though you may be unaware of it, you are thinking. Grief comes from your thoughts about the one you lost—thoughts about the future without this person and thoughts about this intruder we call grief. Your feelings could intensify because of the surprise and shock you experience over the onset of intense emotions. And all these intense feelings make you wonder if you're going crazy. It's like a mighty hurricane blowing through your life. But before all the feelings, you may experience something else.

Whether the death is expected or sudden, you may experience numbness. The more unexpected and traumatic the loss, the more intense your numbness will be. At first the feelings are muted like muting the sound on your TV. The initial shock of knowing a loved one is dead puts most into a paralyzing state of shock. "This is a period in which no mourner can describe clearly, thanks to nature's protection measures. Afterward, looking back, it is recalled as through a rolling mist which thins out occasionally to permit short glimpses of a distant blurred landscape, partly in sun and partly in blackest shadows. Possibly the key word here is *shock*."[3]

Shock is like a breaker box in a house. When you have too many lines plugged into the same outlet, the electricity goes out. When you are overloaded by grief, your mind goes into a state of shock that allows you to keep going until you reset the "breakers" in your mind. This happens when you begin to experience and process the multiple emotions that hit you.[4]

It's a natural protection as though someone gave you anesthesia. It insulates you from the intensity of your feelings of loss that you have experienced, but it also may prevent you from understanding the full experience of the loss. This absence is unnerving and brings a sense of unreality. And you may find yourself wandering around aimlessly. How long will this last? It could be hours, days, or weeks. No one else can tell you. Some say they're living in a dreamlike state.

If you didn't experience numbness or shock, don't be alarmed. We all respond differently. Whatever your initial reaction, it's just the introduction to a new play or drama in your life. The next scene will be the most intense.

CHAPTER 8

The Questions of Grief

❧

The next scenes or groupings of your feelings could be described as a time of *suffering* and *disorganization* or even *chaos*. The trance is over. We will talk about scenes rather than stages, for stages vary depending on whom you read. And there are those who bypass some stages. After the numbness wears off, the pain of separation comes. Sometimes you may wish you could go back to the initial stage of numbness or shock. At least there the pain wasn't so intense. There is an intense longing for the return of the person you lost—for the sight of them, the sound of them, their smell, and just knowing he or she could walk through that door again. One person described the loss of a loved one as "like a having a tree that has been growing in one's heart yanked out by its roots, leaving a gaping hole or wound."[1] And a question begins to form on your lips—Why?

You may be asking why? countless times a day right now. You may be shouting it and shaking your fist, or you may not be asking why? Either way is all right. You may wonder, *Do I have the right to ask why?* Who is to say you don't have the right? Regardless of what you hear, you will probably ask. Job asked the question sixteen times. Others asked as well. *Why* is not just a question—it's a heart-wrenching cry of protest. It's the reaction of "No, this shouldn't be! It isn't right!" Others asked. Listen to their cry.

My God, my God, why have you forsaken me?
(Matt. 27:46)

Why, O LORD, do you stand far off? Why do you hide yourself in times of trouble? (Ps. 10:1)

How long, O LORD? Will you forget me forever?
How long will you hide your face from me?
How long must I wrestle with my thoughts
    and every day have sorrow in my heart?
How long will my enemy triumph over me?
(Ps. 13:1–2)

Ken Gire writes: "Painful questions, all of them. Unanswered questions, many of them. And we, if we live long enough and honestly enough, one day we will ask them, too."[2]

You could be asking them even now.

"Why?" is saying "I need some explanation. I need some answers." Having no answer can feed our anger. There is another side question to this issue. Would any answer suffice at this time? Is there any answer that would put the question to rest? More than likely the answer is, "No, not really." Answers don't always make the pain go away. But don't let others keep you from voicing your pain. Don't be offended by their answers. Even though they don't know the answer, they may be trying to help you.

Keep asking because in time a transformation of your question could occur. One day your why will turn into "What can I do to grow through this experience?" and "How will my life be stronger now?" Faith is involved in this process. On one hand you will ask why and on the other hand say, "I will *learn* to live by faith." Faith is many things. It is not knowing the answer to the why and being willing to wait for an answer. Eventually you may say, "I really don't need the answer in order to go on." Some say not knowing makes recovery difficult, but could it be that knowing could make it even more difficult? We hope an explanation will lessen the hurt. It won't. Job asked and asked and asked again, but the silence of God was loud. Habakkuk, the prophet, cried out and asked why, but the silence of God was loud. Even though Habakkuk never received an answer, he came to the place of acceptance:

> Though the fig tree does not bud
> and there are no grapes on the vines,
> though the olive crop fails
> and the fields produce no food,
> though there are no sheep in the pen
> and no cattle in the stalls,
> yet I will rejoice in the LORD.
> I will be joyful in God my Savior,
> (Hab. 3:17–18)

Ken Gire said, "In times of upheaval, a voice from heaven says, 'Be still and know that I am God.' It doesn't say, 'Be still and know why.' In a distant day the gradual sacrament of understanding may be offered to us."[3]

Accepting the silence could be one of your steps in moving on.

According to Craig Barnes, "God is often silent when we prefer that he speak, and he interrupts us when we prefer that he stay silent. His ways are not our ways.

"To live with the sacred God of creation means that we conduct our lives with a God who does not explain himself to us. It means that we worship a God who is often mysterious—too mysterious to fit our formulas for better living."[4]

In spite of lingering questions, it is still possible to worship God. It is possible to recognize God for who he is and still say, "Why?" "I don't like this." "Answer me!" "Where were you?" and "I don't understand. Help me!"

The struggle to pray at this time is not unusual. But at times it's as though the words stick in your mind and can't get past your lips. The questions, concerns, pleas, and requests are there, but somehow they're derailed in your attempt to express them to God. You may know how to pray but not at this time. You may just sit and say, "Oh God, oh Jesus," again and again. Your suffering has overridden your ability to pray. Paul talked about this. During times like these

God not only knows and understands your hurts and desires but provides the Holy Spirit to intercede for you "with groans that words cannot express" (Rom. 8:26).

Here is a prayer from centuries ago that may help you face each day. Others have said it's helpful to pray this out loud.

> I arise today
> through God's strength to pilot me:
> God's might to uphold me,
> God's wisdom to guide me,
> God's eye to look before me,
> God's ear to hear me,
> God's word to speak for me,
> God's hand to guard me,
> God's way to lie before me,
> God's shield to protect me.
> —St. Patrick, 433

Your feelings will come and go often for some unknown reason. At other times they will erupt because of some triggers that activated them. Being around certain people will give you a sense of comfort and safety, whereas with others you may experience tension. Going to certain stores, restaurants, or even driving on a certain street can bring back the loss and sadness. These are triggers, and often they are sights, sounds, and even smells. Understanding which ones trigger pleasant or unpleasant memories and emotions can help you know what to move toward and what to move away from during this journey.[5]

CHAPTER 9

The Expression of Tears

In the midst of this turmoil, God has a plan for your pain. It's called tears. We refer to it as crying or weeping. Sometimes we hide our tears or try to block them or apologize for them. But why should we apologize for something that is a gift from God? Perhaps you're one who never learned to cry. Some are afraid to let go with their tears. Fear and reservations block their expression. And if for some reason it happens, they refer to it as, "I broke down." Cars and refrigerators break down; people don't. We shed tears, cry, or weep. We were created to cry. It's a fitting response to sorrow.

Nicholas Wolterstoff, who lost his son to a climbing accident, said, "But why celebrate stoic tearlessness? Why insist on never outwarding the inward when that inward is bleeding? Does enduring not require as much strength as never crying? Must we always mask our suffering? May we not sometimes allow people to see and enter it?"[1]

"How long did Jesus grieve? He wept. He let the pain of the death of his friend Lazarus overcome him. And he knew the separation was temporary. . . . Go on and cry a river. Let it rain down like tears from heaven. And let it cleanse and carry you to the arms of those who will be strong for you."[2]

If you try to hold your pain and grief inside, you'll find it's like trying to build a dam across the ocean. Pour out your grief to a trusted friend. Pour it out to God.

When the loss first occurs, you may cry as though the heavens have opened with a forty-day flood. And you think it will never end. One day the clouds part, and there's a bit of rest from the moisture. Then the storms return. It's hard to remember what the sun and stars and sky look like. But little by little they return.[3]

Your tears are not just helpful; they're needed. If you didn't cry, your eyes would be dry, and soon blindness could set in. If you sob and weep, you won't suffer permanent damage; you will live through this pain—if you're allowed to talk about it.[4] Christians grieve over our losses with both real tears and real hope. We rest in what the psalmist said:

> He reached down from on high
>   and took hold of me;
>   he drew me out of deep waters.
> He rescued me from my powerful enemy,
>   from my foes, who were too strong for me.
> They confronted me in the day of my disaster,
>   but the LORD was my support.
> He brought me into a spacious place;
>   he rescued me because he delighted in me.
> (Ps. 18:16–19)

Do you hear how God regards you? He not only loves you; he delights in you. During your darkest hour hold on to those words. Not only that but God moves "near to the brokenhearted, and saves those who are crushed in spirit" (Ps. 34:18 NASB).

Many of your tears will be for yourself, but they will also include other family members and friends. This can add to your own burden. Max Lucado describes our tears:

> Tears.
>
> Those tiny drops of humanity. Those round, wet balls of fluid that tumble from our eyes, creep down our cheeks, and splash on the floor of our hearts. They were there that day. They are always present at

such times. They should be; that's their job. They are
miniature messengers; on call twenty-four hours a
day to substitute for crippled words. They drip, drop
and pour from the corner of our souls, carrying with
them the deepest emotions we possess. They tumble
down our faces with announcements that range
from the most blissful joy to darkest despair.

The principle is simple; when words are most
empty, tears are most apt.[5]

So much is distilled in our tears, not the least of which
is wisdom in living life. From my own tears I have learned
that if you follow your tears, you will find your heart. If you
find your heart, you will find what is dear to God. And if
you find what is dear to God, you will find the answer to
how you should live your life.[6]

A promise for your future is found in Psalm 126:5-6:
> Those who sow in tears
> > will reap with songs of joy.
> He who goes out weeping,
> > carrying seed to sow,
> will return with songs of joy,
> > carrying sheaves with him.

Some have found help in this Prayer for Courage:
> Help me, O God.
>
> Give me the courage to cry.
> Help me to understand that tears bring
> > freshly washed color arching across the soul,
> > colors that wouldn't be there apart from the
> > > rain.
>
> Help me to see in the prism of my tears,
> > something of the secret of who I am.

> Give me the courage
>> not only to see what those tears are revealing
>> but to follow where they are leading.
>
> And help me to see,
>> somewhere over the rainbow,
>> that where they are leading me home.[7]

If others attempt to guide the conversation away from your loss or don't seem to know what to say when you cry, you could simply suggest that it's all right to bring up the subject and talk about it. Your mind fluctuates from being blank to thinking again and again about the one you lost. They come to mind hundreds of times. You feel as though your mind is talking.

Your mind may be flooded by images you can't stop. It's as though your mind won't stop talking to the person. As this happens, begin to discover what is triggering the thoughts. Sometimes the more you try to fight them, the more they persist. Give yourself permission for them to exist, for in time they'll diminish. This process of ruminating is part of your healing and recovery. You feel especially needy at this time, almost impoverished.

What do you need most at this time? Someone to listen, just to be there to hold you, talk to you, go somewhere with you. Everyone needs something. Let others know what you need. They may even cry with you. And remember, one day there will be no more need for tears. "He will wipe every tear from their eyes. There will be no more death or mourning or crying or pain, for the old order of things has passed away" (Rev. 21:4).

CHAPTER 10

New Uninvited Guests

During this time one of the clusters of feelings to emerge will be a sense of *emptiness, loneliness,* and even *isolation.* It feels like there's an empty house both inside and outside of you. And to add to the pain is the sense of isolation even when others are next to you. Invisible boundaries have been erected.

Loneliness is a product of loss. Doug Manning described it in this way: "The awful loneliness seems to be there every moment of every day. The finality of death leaves a hollow feeling all over your body. Loneliness comes in only one size—extra large."[1] In a way your world is depleted. It's collapsed. It's accentuated by others when they fail to hear your cries and requests, being misunderstood and even ignored. The latter often occurs after the initial three months when others think you're doing all right or "should be."

Loneliness brings with it another feeling of not belonging. Those whom you and your loved one socialized or fellowshipped with may not respond to you as much or extend invitations as they once did. You may feel like a fifth wheel and even isolated at times.

Most who lose a loved one are thrust into unknown territory. They may have been through difficult times before and weathered the upsets. Death is terrain most of us don't know about, a wilderness so vast and rugged that you lose all sense of direction.

Many say they are just lost in a wilderness with no recognizable landmarks. How can you survive? By remembering one thing—you're not alone. You may feel lonely, but you're not alone.

Gregory Floyd, who lost a six-year-old son, describes their feelings and thoughts:

> We knew we were not alone. The God of Jesus Christ, who spoke not a word because he knows we could not hear one, was with us like the air we breathe, a vast presence, subtle, but nonetheless so real and fine. We did not need him to say anything. We needed him just to hold us, to hear our heart break again and again, to tell him how unbearable this was and that if he did not shoulder the burden we would be lost. He was always there. The psalmist says, ". . . I am always with you; you take hold of my right hand" (Ps. 73:23 NASB). Touch was what was needed, not words. Yes, hold my right hand, and my left one, too. In the crush of your neck, oh great God.[2]

How do you need to be touched today? Tell God. Ask him. Hold out your arms to him. Let others know you need them to hold you as well.

CHAPTER II

The Invasion of Fear and Anxiety

♣

The second common cluster is *fear* and *anxiety*. And the fears accumulate. They may come and go or be a constant sense of dread. It's a common response whenever we face the unknown and the unfamiliar. They range from the fear of being alone, fear of the future, the fear of additional loss, the fear of desertion or abandonment.

"What will I do?" is a phrase that expresses fear. The greater your emotional investment in the one you lost, the more you'll tend to feel like a ship cut loose to drift at sea. Your anxiety level could be quite intense the more you wonder, "What will happen to me?" "Can I handle this pain?" "What am I to do?" And this leads into the fear of the future. The death of a loved one makes most of life less safe. You may ask, "Where is this fear coming from?" Not all feelings can be explained. And most of these feelings won't last.

You may wake up and ask, "How can I face the day without them?" Those who grieve are afraid of being on their own. There may be anxiety over dealing with the pain of the separation. You may be upset over the realization that you're a different person. You're "without" someone. Many worry over how other family members will cope and survive. And if you lost this one, what if you lose another family member or friend, especially if this loss was sudden and unexpected.

It's common for a major loss to activate memories of earlier losses. And if those early losses weren't grieved over, the residue of accumulated pain may come back along with your current pain. At some point during the process of recovery, reflect on the question, "What else is there in my life that I've never fully grieved over?" Whatever you discover, take what you've discovered during this loss and work on your other losses.

One of the causes of fear and anxiety is grief itself. It's different and intense. You've lost control of your life, and that creates fear. What worked for you before isn't working now, and this too creates fear. The higher the expectations you have for yourself, the greater your need for control; the more perfectionistic you are, the greater your feeling of loss of control and panic. Grief isn't logical. It's not predictable. And so you may be afraid of being consumed by your grief.

Some feel, "I'm losing who I am." It's true. Earlier we mentioned your identity is changing, and this creates confusion. The validation you received from the other is gone. It won't return. Part of you dies in addition to losing your loved one, so you end up grieving for yourself as well.

There is yet another source of fear, "How do I grieve?" We've not been taught how to act or feel in grief in our society. We have few role models or guidelines for those in mourning. So this uncertainty increases fears and insecurities.[1]

The Word of God gives us direction, "I cried out to the LORD in my suffering, and he heard me. He set me free from all my fears" (Ps. 34:6 NLT).

"When anxiety was great within me, your consolation brought joy to my soul" (Ps. 94:19).

CHAPTER 12

What Do I Do with My Guilt?

❧

Guilt and *shame* walk their way into the grief process. There are numerous sources for the guilt. The most immediate guilt comes from taking some responsibility for the loss, or perhaps the guilt is connected to a discussion that you feel contributed to the loss in some way. It could also be leftover unfinished business that you wish you had attended to, and this leads to regrets.

Some continue to live in the land of regrets and let their life become a series of continuous self-recriminating statements. And the regrets seem to grow. They tie into shoulds as well. It could be: "I regret not spending enough time with you, . . . not buying you . . . , . . . not saying I love you enough."

Identify the regrets, write them down, say them out loud, say you are sorry, ask God to take them off your heart and mind, and move on. You can do this.

Guilt may occur because of unresolved negative feelings in a relationship. You may experience guilt over things you did or didn't do. It's common in the early phases of grief to recall all that was negative in your relationship with the one you lost while failing to remember the positives equally as well. There is another tendency as well at this time. You will probably dwell on all the bad or negative things you think you did in your relationship with the person you lost and at the same time overfocus on all the good things the deceased did. And you may hesitate to verbalize these with a close friend who could help you gain a more balanced perspective on what you are thinking. If this is your situation, make a list about yourself and the other about the areas in which you're not focusing. This can bring a more balanced view and lift some of the guilt.

Be aware of "survivor guilt," feeling quilty because you are still alive while your loved one is gone. Perhaps you inherited something or received benefits or insurance money from this loss, and this may add to guilt. Whenever guilt hits, challenge those thoughts and feelings. When the pangs of guilt hit, evict them. You don't need them as a tenant in your life.[1]

Guilt is an unpredictable emotion, and that in itself creates guilt. Some experience guilt because they're not recovering according to their timetable. This is where "should" and "if only" come into your mind. When a death is unexpected or sooner than anticipated, the tendency to blame rushes to the forefront. After we've blamed, others, it's easy to transfer the blame to ourselves. "If only I had . . ." The list is endless.

We imagine that if we had done something different we could have prevented the death. Do we really have that much power? If we had done something different, could we have changed reality? Aren't we placing a heavy burden on ourselves for the death of our loved one? Most "if onlies" are not true. If any of them are, nothing can be done. They are another expression of "I am hurt" and "I feel anger." Replacing the "if onlies" with these other expressions may drain off the emotion.[2]

If only I had . . .

understood the full extent of the illness.
called the doctor sooner.
treated the one I loved more kindly.

taken better care of him or her.
not lost my temper.
expressed my affection more frequently.

When death comes, life is examined. You become more acutely aware of your failures, real or imagined. You want to rectify past errors. You wish to compensate for the wrongs you have committed.

Some people punish themselves with self-destructive acts, as if to say: "See how much I am suffering. Doesn't this prove my great love?" Self-recrimination becomes a way to undo all the things that make you now feel guilty.

And maybe you were guilty. Perhaps you said things you should not have said. Perhaps you neglected to do things you should have done. But who hasn't? What is past is past. It cannot be changed. You already have too much pain to add to the burden of self-accusation, self-reproach, and self-depreciation.[3]

You may experience the "if onlies" because those around you are unwilling to give you permission to grieve. If guilt is present, realize it won't contribute in any positive manner to your recovery. It's unnecessary. It can also be paralyzing, and it's the emotional area in which many become stuck during their grief journey.

CHAPTER 13

I'm Angry

Another feeling is *anger*. It's a feeling of displeasure, irritation, and protest. In grief it's often a protest, a desire to make someone pay, to declare the unfairness of the death when we're frustrated, hurt, afraid, feeling helpless. Sometimes the anger is expressed like a heat-seeking missile. It can erupt suddenly. There is no warning. No alarms sound. The day has been calm, and then the missile explodes. And there is damage. Another day your anger may be expressed in silent withdrawal. It's subtle, but it's still there. But sometimes the anger is frozen. It's stuck, or it turns against you.

Hurt is a core feeling of loss. It is *pain in the present*. What does it feel like? Sometimes it is sadness, sometimes disappointment, and sometimes depression. But often it's turned into anger. It feels as if you have been depleted. You are drained. You need to cope with hurt by expressing it.

Anger is a response to the hurt or pain. It can be *pain in the past, present,* or *future*. When it is in the past, it is resentment. It's not uncommon to experience these feelings even toward the one who died. When direct expression is blocked, it leaks out and is invested elsewhere. If it is invested against oneself, it can become depression.

Some say, "I am not angry." Perhaps it would be better to say, "I *am* angry" several times aloud or to write it out saying, "I am angry because . . ." This may be a better indicator for you.

Is anger necessary? It's not wrong. Had you ever considered the idea that anger is not sin but emotional information? It's one of the many expressions of grief. It's there for a purpose. Because we believe the tragedy or crisis shouldn't have happened, we look for something or someone to blame—a doctor, a hospital, an organization, a CEO, an accountant, a bus driver, or anyone we perceive as having somehow participated in the crisis. Sometimes our anger is vented toward anyone who is around, especially family members. You may be angry at everyone around you who hasn't lost anyone and their lives are going on as usual. They have no idea how you feel since they haven't been devastated as you have.

The bereaved get angry at the physician who tried in vain to help a loved one. Fire and flood victims get angry at the police and firefighters who were unable to save their homes. Widows often feel anger toward close family members after the first few weeks of bereavement. They feel overprotected and overcontrolled, or they feel unsupported and disappointed because they expected assistance from others.

We're angry at terrorists and nations who harbor terrorists, and we *should* be angry. You may get angry at those who fail to reach out and support you during your time of trouble. When we hurt, we want to be acknowledged. We don't want to pretend that everything is OK. It isn't. In some cases it never will be the same. Of course, part of the reason we end up feeling isolated is because no one has taught us how to minister to one another during a time of need.

Sometimes you may feel anger at the one who died. Survivors sometimes feel deserted or victimized. The loss of a spouse or a parent may leave you with the responsibility of what they left undone. Often anger comes because we feel out of control, powerless, and victimized. And we say, "Why didn't I . . . ?" Sometimes we end up being angry at ourselves.

It may be especially hard to admit being angry at God.
Your anger may be at God for not responding in the way
you wanted or anger because your faith and beliefs didn't
seem to work. The distress over the failure of God to
respond in the way you needed him can prolong your grief.
Tell God your feelings. Anger at God is part of the Jewish
tradition. The psalms of lament contain anger at God for
numerous reasons. The anger of grief directed at God is your
response to loss, not a lack of faith. It may be difficult to
accept.

Angry at God

> I told God I was angry.
> I thought He'd be surprised.
> I thought I'd kept hostility
> quite cleverly disguised.
>
> I told the Lord I hate Him.
> I told Him that I hurt.
> I told Him that He isn't fair,
> He's treated me like dirt.
>
> I told God I was angry
> but I'm the one surprised.
> "What I've known all along," He said,
> "you've finally realized.
>
> "At last you have admitted
> what's really in your heart.
> Dishonesty, not anger
> was keeping us apart.
>
> "Even when you hate Me
> I don't stop loving you.
> Before you can receive that love
> you must confess what's true.

"In telling Me the anger
you genuinely feel,
it loses power over you,
permitting you to heal."

I told God I was sorry
And He's forgiven me.
The truth that I was angry
has finally set me free.
                              —Jessica Shaver[1]

You will want to use your anger creatively. You don't want it to use you or to dominate your life. Ignoring it or telling it to go away won't work. Judging it and telling yourself it is wrong won't help at this time. Turning its energy into a gift to do something constructive will work. This is far better than letting it soak and seethe in bitterness and resentment. These feelings can destroy you as well as relationships. The best person to tell about your anger is God. He wants to hear it unedited from you. There are creative ways for you to express your anger. Many have found it beneficial to keep a prayer journal. As you write, you will discover more about your anger and yourself than you thought possible. What you write in a journal you don't take out on family or friends. Don't be surprised if you discover during this process that your anger is covering other emotions. Anger may be safer for you than fear, hurt, or guilt.

Some find it helpful to take a piece of paper and write, "Today I feel angry." They then roll it up and place it in a balloon, blow it up, and then bounce the balloon in the air for several minutes. You keep your anger balloon from hitting the ground. Then write how you feel after doing this.

Anger is all right as long as it doesn't get the best of you. It will never get the best of God. Your feelings may be like the psalmist:

How long, O LORD? Will you forget me forever?
How long will you hide your face from me?

How long must I wrestle with my thoughts
    and every day have sorrow in my heart?
    How long will my enemy triumph over me?
Look on me and answer, O LORD my God.
    Give light to my eyes, or I will sleep in death.
    (Ps. 13:1–3)

In time give up your anger. It has its purpose, but it will outlive its purpose. In spite of all David's angry questions, he came to this place:

But I trust in your unfailing love;
    my heart rejoices in your salvation.
I will sing to the LORD,
    for he has been good to me. (Ps. 13:5–6)

CHAPTER 14

Will the Sadness Ever Go Away?

❧

Finally, there is the sense of *sadness, depression,* and *despair.* When you are sad, you're yearning for whom you lost. Depression makes each day look as though the dark clouds are here to stay. Apathy blankets you like a shroud, and withdrawal becomes a lifestyle. When depression hits, your perspective leaves. Depression will alter your relationships because you're oversensitive to what others say and do. Jeremiah the prophet displayed the feelings: "Desperate is my wound. My grief is great. My sickness is incurable, but I must bear it" (Jer. 10:19 TLB).

The deeper your depression, the more paralyzing is your sense of helplessness. You feel passive and resigned. Everything seems out of focus. You feel as though you're in a deep, dark pit, cold and isolated. There doesn't seem to be a way out of this pit either. Depression can blind you to the realities of life. It narrows your perception of the world. You end up feeling all alone, as though no one else cares about you.

Depression affects you spiritually and can change the way you see God. It's hard to believe in a loving and personal God who knows the answers and wants you to succeed and yet seems to be far off. The psalmist reflected these feelings as well:

> Lord, be kind to me because I am weak.
>> Heal me, Lord, because my bones ache.
> I am very upset.
>> Lord, how long will it be?
> Lord, return and save me.
>> Save me because of your kindness.
> Dead people don't remember you.
>> Those in the grave don't praise you.
> I am tired of crying to you.
>> Every night my bed is wet with tears.
>> My bed is soaked from my crying.
> My eyes are weak from so much crying.
>> They are weak from crying about my enemies.
> (Ps. 6:2–7 NCV)

In place of experiencing peace and joy, the light of God in your life, you feel just the opposite. You feel empty. Often Christians who are depressed feel even worse because of their false beliefs about depression. *It is not a sin for a Christian to be depressed.* And most of our depression is not brought on by sin.

Many people are surprised to read the account of Jesus' depression in the garden of Gethsemane. Jesus was the perfect man and free from all sin, yet complete in his humanity and tempted as we are. Look at the account in Matthew 26:36–38 (AMP):

> Then Jesus went with them to a place called Gethsemane, and He told His disciples, Sit down here while I go over yonder and pray. And taking with Him Peter and the two sons of Zebedee, He began to show grief and distress of mind and was deeply depressed. Then He said to them, My soul is very sad and deeply grieved, so that I am almost dying of sorrow. Stay here and keep awake and keep watch with Me.

Jesus knew what was about to happen to him, and it depressed him. He did not feel guilty over being depressed.

Neither should we. But our depression creates a distortion of life and intensifies any guilt feelings we have. Thus, guilt over depression leads to more depression!

If you tend toward depression even before experiencing a crisis, then your depression will be intensified during a crisis. The feeling of despair is such a major loss that the future looks dismal. A sense of hopelessness has invaded your life. Despair brings a sense of meaningless and worthlessness to life.

Some have said there is a "psalm for every sigh" we express. More than half of the psalms are laments. These psalms wrestle with God's presence and absence and his loyal, faithful love. You may feel what these writers said:

> You are God my stronghold.
>> Why have you rejected me?
> Why must I go about mourning,
>> oppressed by the enemy? (Ps. 43:2)

> Has his unfailing love vanished forever?
>> Has his promise failed for all time?
> Has God forgotten to be merciful?
>> Has he in anger withheld his compassion?
> (Ps. 77:8–9)

> You have put me in the lowest pit,
>> in the darkest depths.
> Your wrath lies heavily upon me;
>> you have overwhelmed me with all your
>>> waves. (Ps. 88:6–7)

Like grief, depression is a journey, but it feels more like a passage through an arid desert than a lush forest. It's a long, exhausting trek through a barren land. Others have traveled this way. The Israelites learned to know God through their desert discomfort. In the midst of emotional despair, you too can experience the living God.[1]

You are not alone in your sadness. Jesus himself was described as "a man of sorrows, and acquainted with grief" (Isa. 53:3 KJV). Nancy Guthrie, after the loss of two of her children, wrote: "And so it is in our sadness that we discover a new aspect of God's character and reach a new understanding of Him that we could not have known without loss. He is acquainted with grief. He understands. He's not trying to rush us through our sadness. He's sad with us."[2]

A phrase in a psalm can be a source of comfort, especially during those bleak lonely moments: "Why are you in despair, O my soul? And why have you become disturbed within me? Hope in God, for I shall again praise Him for the *help of His presence*" (Ps. 42:5 NASB, author's italics).

It reminds us that God is present. There is never a moment that he isn't walking with us. In grief we feel isolated, alone. When we focus on that feeling, we forget that we are never, ever alone. It may help to say, "God, you say you are present. I don't feel your presence. I feel your absence. God, work on my mind so I remember that you *are* present, and in time I may feel your presence. But right now I need the knowledge."

Remember another psalm: "I sought the LORD, and He answered me, and delivered me from all my fears. . . . The LORD is near to the brokenhearted and saves those who are crushed in spirit" (Ps. 34:4, 18 NASB).

Remember Jesus' promise: "I tell you the truth, you will weep and mourn while the world rejoices. You will grieve, but your grief will turn to joy" (John 16:20).

CHAPTER 15

What Do I Do with My Feelings?

♣

Some have said grief is the blackest night of confusion because of all the emotions. Your range of feelings is like a smorgasbord. Each day you have a wide variety to choose from. There will also be daily variations. They come and they go. You may think they're gone for good, but not so—they come and go and overlap one another. Over time they're less frequent and less intense.

Perhaps the best way to deal with emotions that invade your life is to follow the example of a hiker who had just read the Forest Service instructions of what to do when encountering wild animals, especially mountain lions. This man was jogging with his dog and came upon a mountain lion. The lion began stalking the man and then ran after him. Fortunately, the man remembered what he had read. He stopped, turned around, and faced the mountain lion. The lion wasn't expecting this, so it stopped and walked away. Your emotions are like that mountain lion. Face them head-on, listen to their message, and eventually you'll rise above them.

When we lose a loved one, we sometimes believe that God has abandoned us. He hasn't. When we lose a loved one, we sometimes feel as if nothing matters—but it does. When we lose a loved one, we sometimes think life is not worth living. It is!

In times of loss and sorrow, we people of faith have to "believe against the grain." In our weakness God reveals his strength, and we can do more than we thought possible.

Faith means clinging to God in spite of our circumstances. It means following him when we can't see him. It means being faithful to him when we don't feel like it.

Resilient people have a creed that says, "I believe!" and they affirm their creed daily. In essence they say:

- I believe God's promises are true.
- I believe heaven is real.
- I believe God will see me through.
- I believe nothing can separate us from God's love.
- I believe God has work for me to do.

"Believing against the grain" means having a survivalist attitude. Not only can we survive, but out of it we can create something good.[1] We need to cry out, "God help me believe!"

Your thoughts are not immune from grief. You may not like some of your thoughts. You would like more control of them, but that's difficult. The preoccupation you have with the death and your pain can occur when you're in a group, attempting to work through a business transaction, or when you're driving—which could lead to a ticket or an accident. Sometimes you may feel as though you've become obsessive with your thoughts since you can't let go of them. You're not. These too will diminish.

It's true that feelings can be held back and bottled up. But not for long. If you don't let them out, you'll discover they'll find their own means of expression. Your storage space is only so large. It has limits. And when it's full, feelings spill out causing confusion, turmoil, or a rash of physical ailments.

Putting your feelings and thoughts into words gives them shape and meaning. Expressing them to others means you're not having to carry their weight by yourself. It also gives you a freedom to overcome them. Sometimes it provides you with the freedom to be free of them. If you don't give them a voice, they will still find a way. Often they explode. For many, giving these a written expression defuses their intensity.

There is another reason for your expression of feelings. It's a message to everyone around you of how you're doing. If you are silent, others will think "you're getting over it" and doing just fine. Your display of grief needs to be clear. Most won't know what you need unless you tell them. Be specific. Avoid words like, "I'm OK," or "I'm fine." Others can't read your mind. If you're struggling, say so. If you're depressed, tell them. If you can't function, describe it. Don't hesitate to say, "I could use your help in this way." If another just quotes a verse or says she'll pray for you, say, "Thank you, but here is something else you could do that would be helpful."

There is something else you can do: Share with your friends and family the book or video *Tear Soup*. Ask them to purchase a copy for you and watch the video together. It *will* change their response to you (see the Appendix).

Even though you can't schedule your grief, you may want to select some time and solitude in your life that is purposeful. It may be a time when you choose to vent all of your feelings, sit and weep, reflect on the future, listen to worship music, consider forgotten blessings, or simply stare into space.

The experience of this woman may reflect where you are:

I cry from time to time, and often find myself swallowing this strange lump in my throat. But I am learning not to apologize for my tears since they are God's gracious gift to me to express my loss, and a sign that I am indeed recovering. As I continue to *feel,* God continues to *heal.*

At times, I feel so angry and irritable for no apparent reason. Most of the time I just don't have a tangible reason, and this causes me much frustration. One thing I have learned is that *all* of my emotions have greatly intensified during this time of grieving. The loss of my parents brought with it a multitude of other losses as well. The loss of what never was and will never be (on this side of heaven). But I continue to pray that God will turn these losses for his gain.

During this year grief has affected every part of my being—physically (some days my body ached from the inside out), emotionally (at times I felt completely numb, and other days I felt raw to the touch), intellectually (some days my memory was so bad I feared I was in the beginning stages of dementia), relationally (retreating and withdrawing was safe), and spiritually (some days feeling the absence of God felt too much for me to bear). So, if I don't always make sense, please forgive me and be patient with me. Just a few months ago, I found myself standing in Starbuck's when a kind employee called out, "Have a nice day," to which I replied, "Vacuum." We looked at each other with great bewilderment![2]

Listen to what Elisabeth Eliot learned through the loss of her husband: "We are not given explanations, but to hearts open to receive it, a more precious revelation of the heart of our loving Lord."

As you express your emotions of grief, remember the following:

> But it hurts. . . . Differently
> there's no way to predict
> how you will feel.

> The reactions of grief are
> not like recipes,
> with given ingredients
> and certain results.

Each person mourns in a
different way.

You may cry hysterically
or
you may remain outwardly controlled,
showing little emotion.

You may lash out in anger against
your family and friends,
or
you may express your gratitude
for their dedication.

You may be calm one moment—
in turmoil the next.

Reactions are varied and
contradictory.

Grief is universal

At the same time it
is extremely personal.

Heal in your own way.[3]

With such a jumbled array of feelings, no wonder
there's a sense of confusion.

The following Ball of Grief describes the normal array
of feelings you may experience:

Ball of Grief

Take out your, *Ball of Grief*, each day. Some days
it seems that each one belongs to you. Yet another
day one or two are dominating your life. You're not
unusual. This is the way of grief. Share your Ball of
Grief with others so they can understand. It may
help them with their own grief.

GRIEF...

A TANGLED 'BALL' OF EMOTIONS

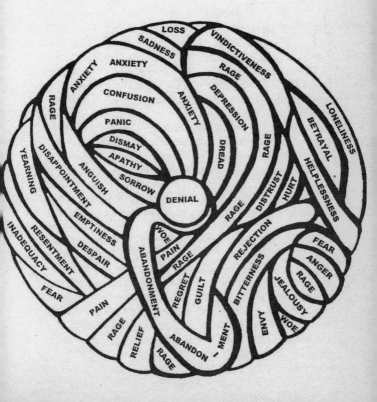

CHAPTER 16

The Feeling No One Talks About

One of the secret feelings of grief is relief. Few would admit to this. It's an "I shouldn't be experiencing this" type of feeling mixed in with all the other responses.

Some individuals who die were more unloved than loved. But rarely does anyone ever talk about them in this way, especially after they die. Sometimes when a family member dies, a person experiences feelings they weren't supposed to, like relief, and sometimes there's a sense of freedom and peace. For some it's a mixture of feelings, but for others these are the dominating ones.

Many people lived in bondage to their parents or spouse for years. Abusive or alcoholic relationships were the secret they lived with, but when death came, so did liberation. It could have been a caregiving situation for many years with a loved one who was disabled in some way or terminally ill. Sometimes the deceased wanted to die to be out of their pain and experience a new relationship in heaven. When you care for someone close to you and you see them suffering or deteriorating, you want them to be free of it by dying. The end of suffering sets the loved one free, but it also sets the caregiver free in many ways. Sometimes the freedom is in finances, time, decisions, or new relationships. But rarely does anyone talk about this for concern of what others might think.[1]

You end up feeling dual relief if you were a caregiver. But sometimes the relief is relationship relief when you've lived with criticism, abuse, oppression, or anxiety. If you lived in a relationship where you were constantly threatened, humiliated, and mistreated, relief is the natural result.[2] Sometimes you experience guilt because of this feeling but perhaps not.

If others say, "You must be so relieved," you may hesitate to admit it. Relief is not the same as saying you are glad your loved one is dead. It's more of the lifting of a burden that had no other way of changing. It's not a betrayal or disloyalty or a character fault in you. It's a normal response. Your relief from the burden of feeling relieved comes from admitting it first to yourself. It helps to say it aloud or write it out several times and then share it with a friend who is a good listener and understands. These are not feelings to be hidden away, for they will grow in secret. It's all right to take a sigh of relief as one of a number of emotions you feel.

When a relationship has been difficult over the years, many end up feeling as if they were living a lie. They put on a positive face for years and lied to others but also lied to themselves about their own needs. When death is a relief, grievers may not have the opportunity to process their grief in the way that works best: telling and retelling their story. When you can talk about your loss in the presence of others, you can sort out your feelings. When you are emotionally fragile after a death, the last thing you want is the reaction and censure of another who is taken back by your feelings of relief.[3]

And if a relationship was bad and there's relief, there is also grief. But the grief may be over what you didn't have in the relationship and would never be possible in the future.[4] And in bad relationships, relief may occur, but often there is a lingering residue that may take work for it to go away.

CHAPTER 17

Complicated Deaths

The loss of a loved one by natural death is difficult enough. But many losses go far beyond this. When a death occurs and you never had a chance to say good-bye, your grief will be more intense and last longer.

When a loved one dies suddenly of an illness no one knew about, it comes as a shock because there is no time for preparation. It's a time when many major decisions need to be made, yet the emotional surge you experience makes it difficult to make decisions. Sudden illness or death robs you of saying good-bye as well as gaining some closure in the relationship. You end up with a multitude of unanswered questions, but there's not much you can do. Sudden death also occurs when a loved one who was expected to die does so months before they were supposed to.

You see, the way in which our loved one died will have a powerful effect on how we grieve:

Sudden deaths, especially violent or accidental deaths, provoke our greatest shock, anxiety and distress. Violent deaths make us feel vulnerable and fearful. Such deaths may provoke our rage or indignation at the injustice of the death. Suicide, too, has a tragic, shocking quality. Suicide may arouse unfounded guilt or a sense of failure among the survivors.

Peaceful, sudden deaths, such as dying in one's sleep, seem more like a blessing, for we imagine this as an easy passage for the deceased. However, any sudden death provokes many questions, doubts and concerns. We wonder why the death happened. Who is to blame? Could it have been prevented? Sudden deaths feel unnatural. We preoccupy ourselves with "if only," ruminations in which we try to rewrite history to erase this disaster. Because we are so unprepared for loss in a sudden death, and because we usually have so much unfinished business with the deceased, sudden deaths seem to be the hardest with which to cope.[1]

WHEN YOUR LOSS IS SUDDEN

The shock of a sudden, unexpected death puts you at a high risk for a pattern of complicated grieving. Why does this happen? How does this affect your life when your capacity to cope crumbles due to a sudden loss?

- Your loss makes no sense whatsoever. No one can explain it adequately.
- You can't even say good-bye or finish any unfinished business. It's difficult to find closure to your relationship.
- Your emotional reactions are heightened much more than when a natural death occurs.
- Your symptoms of grief and shock persist, and this in turn can demoralize you.
- You may tend to hold yourself responsible more than you normally would.
- You experience a profound loss of security and confidence in your world. In fact, you are shattered.
- You may tend to focus on the negative aspects of the relationship with the deceased rather than having a balanced view.
- You have other sudden major losses because of the unexpectedness of the loss.

All of these factors could lead you to experience post-traumatic stress disorder.[2]

If the death of your loved one was one of violence, you have other painful questions running through your mind such as "Were they aware of what was going to happen?" or "Were they in pain?" Your mind tries to focus on the act itself.

If the death was due to murder or suicide, your grief is even greater because of your outrage over the act. Sometimes the strong desire we have for more details or wanting to see the body or the site prolongs the shock and pain.

An experience even worse is not knowing what happened. Sometimes a death leaves many unanswered questions. For some reason we seem to feel better when we have great detail, as bad as it may be. Perhaps it's because it leaves less room for speculation. We often tend to think the worst.

WHEN YOUR LOSS IS ANTICIPATED

Perhaps you had to watch a lingering death. This is an agonizing experience. It is an almost unbearable experience to see a loved one hurting, and you feel helpless to ease the suffering. You try. You ask. You plead. But you end up feeling helpless. It is hard to live with what feels like a death sentence, followed by a reprieve, followed by another horrendous bout of pain; and this may be repeated again and again during a long illness.

If you were the one who discovered the death, your grief will tend to be complicated. The scene may be frozen in your memory and difficult to let go, especially if this was not expected. All this creates extra issues for you to deal with that other family members or friends don't have to deal with. You may see others moving forward in their grief recovery sooner than you, and you may feel left behind. But your recovery will occur. Others didn't have the burden to carry that you had.

Sometimes there is no body to view or to bury, which can leave you with some doubts. "Did they really die?" "How will I know for sure?" This has happened in many types of accidents, disasters, or battles in war.

These are just some of the complications you may have to face in your journey. If so, I suggest some additional reading to assist you, such as the chapter on "Complicated Grief" in *The Mourning Handbook* by Helen Fitzgerald.[3]

CHAPTER 18

Handling Special Occasions

Grief is difficult. But there is something you need to be aware of that will make it even harder—holidays and special dates such as birthdays and anniversaries. These are predictable times when your grief hurts more. These are grief attacks. All of these special days activate a flood of memories of the way it used to be but won't be again. There will be a vacant place this year and in the future. Many have expressed the desire to bypass these special days or holidays. Unfortunately, they can't be avoided, and even if they could, the pain won't leave. Some prefer to have special occasions stay as they were.

What can be done? Keep in mind that holidays are emotional times for everyone. The past memories and traditions of this day and the sights and sounds will activate a sense of sadness.

Think about how much of this special day you can handle. What has been your role during this day? How might it be different? What are you capable of doing? Let others know you will feel and be different and will be making some changes this year. If you accept invitations to go somewhere, make sure you want to and avoid accepting out of obligation or guilt. Sometimes those in grief are talked into buying, eating, and attending and end up regretting every decision. It's easy to get pressured into pleasing others on these special occasions. What will be best for you is the question to consider. What do you want to do this year?

You will need to make decisions about parties, gifts, cards, etc. Sometimes it helps to write about the upcoming special occasion. Answer questions like, "What should I do about . . . ?" or "What bothers me about this day is . . ." "What I miss most about the one I lost is . . ." "I wish you were here at this time to help me with . . ." You don't have to be concerned about what people will think if you don't attend something, change tradition, or don't send cards. Perhaps one of the best ways to handle this special time will be thinking through what you would prefer doing and then discussing this with other family members to hear their thoughts and share yours. Let extended family know what you will be doing as well. If children are involved, keep their needs in mind since some holidays or occasions may mean more to them than to you.

Two difficult days are birthdays. Will you still do something special on the birthday of the deceased, get together with others, write a letter, or ignore the day? Also consider your own birthday. It could feel especially empty because of the absence. How would you like to spend it? This is something for you to decide.

CHAPTER 19

Capturing the Memories

Many who grieve are upset even more when they discover some of the memories of their loved one begin to fade. The greater the distance in time from being with a person, the more this will occur. One man who lost his wife after thirty-five years made a decision not to let this occur, which many others are now doing for their loss. He decided to write down every thought or memory that came to his mind about his wife until he had accumulated a thousand of them. He called this his collection of a thousand one-liners, which would give him a complete picture. Perhaps something like this would aid you in your quest to remember.

You have stories about your loved one. So do others. Telling all these stories is a wonderful way to celebrate a life and give as complete a picture as possible of who this person was. Some have found it helpful in processing their grief to ask friends and relatives to share one of their favorite stories about the loved one.

One of the new roles you take on after the loss of your loved one is becoming their historian. You may be the main person to convey to others who your loved one really was. Newspapers carry obituaries, but you probably want others to know more than those basic facts. You are the one to decide what you want the world to know about your loved one. You're creating a biography. And it's not just facts. It's who they were as a person. It's an exploration of a life lived rather than a history. It's capturing the important elements of one's life, commemorating who they were, and giving a testimonial about them.

What you say and *how* you say it conveys what this person meant to others. At a time when you're ready, consider this possibility. If you do, write about their life—celebrate their life. Give voice to your precious memories. It's what you saw and knew about this person. And remember, others may have a different perspective since we are all important, hopefully growing throughout our life and gradually being conformed to the image of Christ. You may want to create small vignettes and later weave them together into a more complete story. And most important, even though this is for others, it's for you most of all. It gives expression to what you are attempting to hold on to, clarity to the jumbled mixture of memories, and it preserves what will gradually fade in time.[1]

CHAPTER 20

Recovery—It Will Happen

Recovery—it seems like an elusive dream. It's something most in grief desperately want but wonder if it's attainable. "When will I arrive? When will it happen?" are the concerns. It's not a one-time arrival at a set destination. It's an ongoing process. It started when you began to grieve. It's been going on for some time and will continue. Some days it seems possible, and some days you wonder.

What seems strange now will begin to feel familiar. Right now one of the strongest experiences is the absence of your loved one. It's a hole with sharp, jagged edges. Over the months and years, the edges dull, and the absence begins to become familiar. This, too, is a sign of recovery.

There is another side to grief. It may not be what you expect. It won't be pain free. Life won't be back to normal. It will be different. You will create a new normal. Right now you may be feeling stuck, and it's a feeling worse than being in traffic. For there you know you will eventually find relief. It's more of being mired in quicksand where each step you try to take, you sink deeper. I've been in quicksand before. You feel trapped, and soon panic takes over. With grief it's easy to believe the numbness or pain or sorrow or anger will be your constant life companion. It won't. All that you experience will diminish. But it's like learning to swim. You have to step into the water to begin the process. It's safe on the shore because it's familiar.

The journey of grief will take you through uncharted waters. The unfamiliar, though, will become familiar. It will become your new life. And it's better than remaining frozen with grief. Grief has a beginning, but it also has an end even though it doesn't seem possible.

Everyone seems to ask, "How long will it take?" How long before the grief journey is over? When you ask this question, you're in good company. The psalmists and prophets asked God this same question. We want answers. We want closure. We want to know there is an end in sight. Most want it over in weeks or, at the most, months. It's more likely years. You can't compare yourself with others and their grief. Even within the same family, members grieve differently in expression, intensity, and time.

But, as you consider the question of "How long will it take?" and the overall time frame of grief, there are specific points in time for you to be aware of. The third month after the death is often difficult. The shock and numbness have worn off, and by now it's difficult to deny your loss. Many say it feels just like the first twenty-four hours following the actual loss. After six to nine months, you need to consider the relationship of your emotional and physical health. This is a time when your body's immune system may be weakened even more than the initial month. But if one does the work of grieving and doesn't postpone it or avoid it, the immune deficiency is avoidable.[1]

The first year anniversary is a difficult time. The intensity of grief and pain seems to return to the level it was immediately following the death. And you wonder, *What is wrong with me? Am I losing my mind? Won't I ever get over this?* It's a normal response. And by anticipating this could happen, you won't question yourself as you realize this too is normal.

By the eighteenth month you may find yourself experiencing stretches of time where you may have many more good days than difficult ones. But then you wake up one morning, and the sadness is overwhelming, and all you think about is the one you lost. You've hit a grief bump or detour, and this is normal. Tell yourself this is an indication of progress. It's not a setback, and it won't last long. What can you do? Handle it by doing what you would do if your loss were recent.[2]

You will hear others say, "You need to let go and move on." Their timing in such a suggestion is often off and out of sync with what you need to hear at the time. At first you may bristle at someone else telling you what to do. After all, they're not where you are. But wait, what if *you* told yourself to "pick up the pieces and get on with your life"? What would you do? Which piece would you pick up? That's where it begins, one piece at a time. What can you do today to begin moving on? What will you do tomorrow and the day after?

At some point "letting go" *will* be a step in your grief journey. We resist it because we think it means not caring anymore or blocking out the memories of my loved one. Letting go is not the same as not caring. It doesn't mean not remembering your loved one. You want to do that. You need to, for memories are what you have left. Initially those sharp memories can be painful, but in time they begin to fade, and that in itself can be another loss. No, letting go means taking the energy and emotional investment you had in that relationship and beginning to invest it elsewhere. It's shifting your focus. Letting go is leaving behind the person you lost in such a way that you're free to move on. To let go you need to recognize what needs letting go. It could be regrets, unfulfilled expectations, anger, the lifestyle you used to have, or even a routine. Easy? No. Necessary? Yes. There's an insecurity in letting go but a greater security in embracing life. It's a process that may be repetitive, and some days will seem freer than others. And it occurs when *you* are ready.[3]

CHAPTER 21
Unfinished Issues

In this book issues are mentioned about grief that exist but seem to be avoided. Perhaps it's their sensitive nature, or we're ashamed that these situations or feelings exist. Not addressing them hinders the grieving process. Nothing in our life is hidden from God, for God knows our thoughts as well as what we are going to say before we say it. Nothing surprises him, and he wants us to grieve.

You may be struggling with the issue of unfinished business between you and the one who died. Many have said they felt left dangling with statements unsaid, issues unresolved, and no closure. The person may be gone, but the issues remain, and you're the only one left to try to resolve them. Whatever is unfinished can be a barrier to moving along the path to recovery. Was it a situation unresolved, unfinished discussions, arguments, the failure to give or ask forgiveness, or problems never confronted? Many have stated, "If only I could have said, 'I love you' or 'good-bye' one more time." Or perhaps there were harsh words prior to the death, and you wish more than anything else in the world they could be taken back or erased. You replay the scene again and again, and each time your pain throbs. And so our unfinished business may be regrets as well as other concerns.

What can you do to finish what is unfinished? If this is a concern in your life, instead of carrying this around in your mind and struggling with it, make a list of everything you think was unfinished as well as what you think your loved one would have said was unfinished. As you look at each incident, is there anything you could do to settle the issue? One way is saying, "I'm sorry" out loud or writing a letter. Some draw pictures of what they wish was different. Some place a letter in the casket, at the graveside, at a memorial. It's also important to give yourself permission to have unfinished business like everyone else. It's a matter of saying, "I wish I would have . . . , but I didn't. It's not the end of the world. I can handle the way it turned out. I can go on with my life." If you feel that you need the person's forgiveness, you could still ask for it, but more important is asking God for his forgiveness for any offense. He is the one who gives complete forgiveness and can lift any burden in your life.

Perhaps your unfinished business is clinging to hurts and offenses from the one who died. Some carry videotapes full of pain in their memory. We carry the offenses of the other person in our mind as a burden. We inflict inner torment upon ourselves. There's a solution. Forgive the person. When you release them, you're released. If we don't forgive, we sentence ourselves to the prison of resentment. Lewis Smedes said it well:

> When you forgive someone for hurting you, you perform spiritual surgery inside your soul; you cut away the wrong that was done to you so that you can see your "enemy" through the magic eyes that can heal your soul. Detach that person from the hurt and let it go, the way children open their hands and let a trapped butterfly go free.
>
> Then invite that person back into your mind, fresh, as if a piece of history between you had been erased, its grip on your memory broken. Reverse the seemingly irreversible flow of pain within you.[1]

We are able to forgive because God has forgiven us. He has given us a beautiful model of forgiveness. Allowing God's forgiveness to permeate our lives and renew us is the first step toward wholeness.

CHAPTER 22

Saying Good-bye

❧

One of the steps you can take in the letting go process is writing a "Letting Go" letter. A letter such as this generates feelings but releases them as well. It moves you along the recovery process and brings healing. Some read the letter out loud by themselves or to a trusted friend. You could talk about one of the most special times you ever experienced together, what you miss, what you wish, what you wish you could still talk about, what has been most difficult for you during the time of grief, what you will do to remember them, and what you've learned. These subjects may bring up others. Conclude your letter by stating that you are in the process of letting go and experiencing life again. Remember this is an honest expression. Here is a sample letter:

Dear . . .

This is a strange letter. I never planned to write to you after your death. But your leaving has left a painful hole in my life. I don't like the empty grieving feeling I have inside. I miss you. I miss it all—your voice, your presence, your laughter, your raising your eyebrows, your stubbornness. You know what else I miss? Your dreaming out loud. I miss our dreams and the future we won't have here together. I feel cheated. This was not the time for you to die. Or it wasn't the time I thought you should.

I've cried buckets of tears over you. I've cried for me and raged at you and God and me and everyone else who still has someone. I've wanted you to come to me, and I wish I could come to you. I don't like being alone. Oh, I know there are others around, but they aren't you!

It's been months. I've stabilized now. I'm learning to rest in the hope that someday, some way we will see each other again. I'm taking a big step now. I am taking baby steps to go on with my life. I feel strange saying this to you, but you went away, you were taken from me, but I have been holding on to you. Now I'm letting go to live life again. I have our history together, memories together, and a rich life because of you. Thank you. I'm letting you go, but I will never leave you. I will have to let you go many more times. I know that. I miss you. I love you. You are never forgotten.[1]

Perhaps you've been in your grief for a while. There are two questions that will need to be addressed at some time or another. They are different, even strange. Have you committed yourself to a certain amount of time to grieve? Some do unintentionally, and some do intentionally. You may have heard that it takes two years to grieve if it is a natural death, three for accidental. Don't let any of these suggested time frames dictate your recovery time. Don't set a time frame unless it's all the time you need. Keep it open-ended.

Have you given yourself permission to stop grieving at a given point in time in the future? Think about it. Each person in grief will need to give themselves permission *to* grieve and permission to *stop* grieving. Throughout grief you will say good-bye to the one you lost, and eventually you'll say good-bye to your grief.[2] Remember life is a series of hellos, good-byes, and hellos.

Most good-byes carry a sense of sadness, a feeling of "I wish it wasn't so." Do we ever look forward to good-byes or get used to saying the words? Probably not. Many lead to heartache. The word *good-bye*—originally *"God be with you*" or "*Go with God*"—was a recognition that God was a significant part of the going. Perhaps we have forgotten that along with the journey we gain strength when we remember that the Giver of life is there to protect and console, especially when the good-bye is because of death.[3]

A good-bye creates an empty place in you, which causes you to ask questions that need to be asked. Why suffering? What are my values? What do I believe? How will this good-bye impact my life? How will I be different?

The author of *Praying Our Goodbyes* said:

> We all need to learn to say goodbye, acknowledge the pain that is there for us so we can eventually move on to another hello. When we learn to say goodbye we truly learn how to say to ourselves and to others: Go. God be with you. I entrust you to God. The God of strength, courage, comfort, hope, love is with you. The God who promises to wipe away all tears will hold you close and will fill your emptiness. Let go and be free to move on. Do not keep yourself from another step in your homeward journey. May the blessing of our God be with you.[4]

If your loved one knew Jesus and you know Jesus as your Savior, your good-bye is just for a season. One day you'll say hello again. Your loved one is just going to the banquet table before you. Just imagine your loved one in the presence of Jesus experiencing the joy of his closeness.

What *have* you said good-bye to? What *are* you saying good-bye to? What do you *need* to say good-bye to?

Saying good-bye is one of the significant tasks of grieving. It begins with accepting the reality of your loss, working through your pain, adjusting to life without your loved one, withdrawing your emotional energy from this person and reinvesting it elsewhere, and finally, changing the relationship with your loved one from one of presence to one of memory. And saying good-bye is part of the concluding process.[5]

CHAPTER 23

How Your Life
Will Change

❧

Most traveling the path of grief don't see value in the accompanying suffering. In and of itself suffering doesn't have any value. It is what you do with it that brings value. The suffering you experience at this time can lead to some kind of resurrection within you. Grief can awaken a strength, a dormant talent, a never used ability, a never before discovered perspective on life, a new sense of compassion for the struggles and hurts of others, or a new relationship with God. A time of good-bye forces us to make a change in our life and discover what is unfinished within us. The suffering of grief can become a refinement.[1] A time will come when you discover the refinement—perhaps today or tomorrow—but you will make a discovery.

You are not the only one concerned about your recovery. Others will talk to you about it. They want you to recover but probably sooner than you will. And what they mean by recovery may be different from what actually occurs. They'll probably want you back the way you were. But recovery is more about you learning to live with your loss and adjusting to your new life. You will carry a psychic scar, like a scar following physical surgery. It won't interfere with your life, but under certain conditions it may be noticeable.

Your life is going to be full of changes. It already is. These can be positive or negative, growth producing or limiting. At first your life will be diminished by it, but in time it can be enhanced again. Will this loss eventually be a catalyst for growth or remain mired in grief? Perhaps at this point in time you're questioning whether there will be anything positive coming from this loss. It's all right to question this possibility.

Those who lose a loved one in death and move forward become more aware and more sensitive to the loved ones they still have. They develop a commitment to living life more fully. Values are evaluated, and usually relationships are enhanced. Priorities toward family members are reordered. Many find a new depth to their relationship with God. The energy of pain and rage is directed toward meaningful activities. But all of these positives are a choice. They are the result of a journey, one of pain and growth.

Recovery will *not* mean that you forget your loved one or the life you had together. It doesn't mean that you won't feel pain again; be reminded by songs, sights, or sounds; have a mixture of feelings on holidays; or that you won't mourn any longer. But you have to learn to mourn so it doesn't interfere with your new "normal," your new lifestyle.[2]

The author of *The Empty Chair* said:

God does not want us to forget our past. God does not want us to forget the good times, the hard times, the success, the mistakes. God does not ask that you forget that wonderful, or at times conflictual relationship. The battle is over for your loved one. Death has come. Now you can experience his or her victory of a new life while constructing memories for yourself of your past life with your loved one.[3]

You will always have a relationship with those you lost. Recovery means you will remember them realistically. You will remember the good as well as the bad, the happy and the sad times of your relationship as well. It will be more of a historical remembering rather than an emotional one. Any identification you have with this person is healthy.

When you forget your loss for a while, you won't feel like you are betraying your loved one. You no longer hold on to the pain to stay connected with your loved one. You have healthy amounts of holding on and letting go.[4]

Your emotional energy has been withdrawn from the person to invest elsewhere, and you're comfortable with this. If you and your loved one are believers in Jesus Christ, you look forward to being reunited again someday.

Perhaps you, like others, have questions about recovering. Does it mean forgetting the emotional pain of your loss? Forget? No. There will always be a small core that will emerge at unexpected times for many years. Will you ever be able to move on with your life? Yes. Definitely, yes.

CHAPTER 24

Saying Good-bye to Grief

❧

The disorientation of your grief will diminish. How will you know that your disorientation is about over? Several signs will indicate that you are adjusting and recovering.

One of the first signs is a sense of release. It's a turning about in the focus of your thinking. Instead of your thoughts being locked onto the memories of your loved one or wondering what they would be thinking or doing, it's more of thinking about living your own life now and for the future. You reach out more and feel as though you're living life. As one woman said, "My sorrow now feels less an oppressive weight, more a treasured possession. I can take it out and ponder it, then put it safely and carefully away." Another indication is the renewal of your energy. The fatigue begins to lift. You can renew activities that you wanted to engage in before.

A third change is your ability to make better judgments. It usually takes longer for this to occur than most expect. Decision making involves concentration, and those in grief find this difficult. Thoughts are jumbled, and staying focused is a challenge.

Finally, you find yourself eating and sleeping better. How long does this take? For many adults it seems to take eighteen to twenty-four months before these four indicators are present. But so many factors come into play to affect the amount of time recovery takes.[1] (See chapter 25.)

Many ask for a specific road map for their recovery. Their questions are: What do I do? How will I know that I'm getting there? Here are some guidelines that may help:

- You are able to handle the finality of the death.
- You can review pleasant as well as unpleasant memories.
- You can choose to spend time alone and enjoy it.
- You can go somewhere without crying most of the time.
- You are beginning to look forward to holidays.
- You are able to help others in a similar situation.
- You're able to listen to your loved one's favorite music without pain.
- You can sit through a worship service without crying.
- You can laugh at a joke.
- Your eating, sleeping, and exercise patterns are returning to what they were before the death.
- You can concentrate on reading or watching TV.
- You're no longer tired.
- You can find something to be thankful for.
- You are beginning to build new relationships.
- You are beginning to experience life again.
- You are patient with yourself when you experience a "grief spasm" again.
- You are beginning to discover new personal growth from your grief.[2]

Recovery involves many elements. Your diet is one of them. It may be difficult to eat at this time. Food has lost its taste but not its nutrients. You need a substantial and balanced diet. It doesn't need to have taste at this time. Your throat and stomach may resist but override them.

Exercise is another ingredient. It can reduce your stress and anger. You may need to write yourself a note to remind you or make a commitment with a friend to engage in exercise at least three or four times a week.

Rest and sleep may be a struggle, but because grief drains your energy, you need more of both. Look for various ways to fall asleep. You may need to discuss this with your physician if sleeplessness is an ongoing problem.

Perhaps this picture of recovery has been your experience:

> Recovery from loss is like having to get off the main highway every so many miles because the main route is under construction. The road signs reroute you through little towns you hadn't expected to visit and over bumpy roads you hadn't wanted to bounce around on. You are basically traveling in the appropriate direction. On the map, however, the course you are following has the look of shark's teeth instead of a straight line. Although you are gradually getting there, you sometimes doubt that you will ever meet up with the finished highway. There is a finished highway in your future. You won't know when or where, but it is there. You will discover a greater sense of resilience when you know in advance what you will experience and that you're normal in your response.[3]

And so as you continue in remembering, the pain will subside. Now it may be shouting, but someday it will whisper. The ache in your heart will go away. You may not think this possible at this point in your life, but hearing these words can make this time in your life more bearable. If you are a Christian, your grief is to be different. It's to be infused with hope. The foundation for this hope is found in the death and resurrection of Jesus Christ. "He is the Lord over every loss and every heartache. He is the Lord of all comfort and mercy. He is the Lord of resurrection, restoration and regeneration. He is the Lord of life."[4]

Hope will return to replace the despair. The dust of drought and dark clouds will change. There will be a smile instead of a frown, a calmness instead of being on edge. When? When you've gone through your grief and fulfilled your time. Knowing how long doesn't make it easier. "There is a time for everything, and a season for every activity under heaven: . . . a time to weep and a time to laugh, a time to mourn and a time to dance" (Eccl. 3:1, 4). "The LORD will be your everlasting light, and your days of sorrow will end" (Isa. 60:20).[5]

CHAPTER 25

Trauma—The Deepest Wound

It's been said that it takes two years for the recovery a natural death. Untimely or sudden deaths, the age of the person, the violence of the death, how you heard about the death, or whether you saw it firsthand will intensify the length of recovery. If the death was traumatic for you, the recovery could extend for several years.

It's important for all of us to understand trauma. It's the feeling, "I just can't seem to get over it." When you experience trauma, you feel as out of control as a rider bucked off a horse in a rodeo. A traumatic experience literally disrupts the functioning of your mind and inhibits your ability to reason. It overwhelms your coping ability. It's too much. Trauma shatters your beliefs and assumptions about life, challenges your belief that you have the ability to handle life, and tears apart your belief that the world is safe. Trauma leads to silence; you won't have the words to describe it. Trauma leads to isolation; no one seems to understand the experience you had. Trauma leads to feelings of hopelessness; you feel there was no way to stop what happened or the memories.

SIGNS OF TRAUMA

One of the main indicators that trauma may be part of a person's life is reexperiencing the trauma. Thoughts and pictures of what occurred in the form of dreams, nightmares, or even flashbacks may take up residence in your life. Sometimes they slip into your mind like a video stuck on continuous replay. This sensitivity can become so extreme that an event can trigger a flashback and make you feel and act as if you were experiencing the original trauma all over again. Again and again trauma interrupts life. It stops the normal process of life by its constant intrusion.

In a flashback, it's as though you leave the present and travel back in time to the original event. It seems so real. You see it, hear it, and smell it. Sometimes a person begins to react as if he or she were there. Many times a person is hesitant to admit this to others for fear of their reaction. A flashback is like a cry of something that needs to come out and does so in the only way it knows how. When survivors can talk about the trauma, write about it, and bring it to God in an honest and real way through worship, there isn't as great a need for this memory to be so intrusive in nightmares, images, or flashbacks.

Some reexperience the trauma through dreams, nightmares, or insomnia. A person may shake, shout, or thrash about during the dream. Even though the dream may not be remembered, the terror and fear experienced may be. Sometimes a person reexperiences trauma not through memories or images but through painful and angry feelings that seem to come out of nowhere. These feelings occur because they were repressed at an earlier time. Now the emotions are simply crying out for release.

Another way people reexperience trauma is through numbing and avoidance. It's painful to reexperience trauma. For some, it's agonizing. They want it to go away and disappear forever; but it doesn't, so the body and the mind take over to protect against the pain. This is done by emotional numbing. When numbing occurs, it can create a diminished interest in all areas of life. Some may feel detached from others around them, even the ones they love the most. Often there is no emotional expression because they've shut down everything. They tend to reduce their involvement in life.[1]

Another characteristic of trauma involves a person's increased alertness, usually referred to as hyperalertness or hyperarousal. The strong emotions one experiences—fear, anxiety, anger—affect his or her body, particularly adrenaline output. People who have experienced trauma have their own sets of triggers that can activate the memories of what they experienced. The effort to avoid these situations can make a person a prisoner as well as create difficulty in interpersonal relationships.

If you ended up being traumatized, it's not because of a defect in you. You are not abnormal. The event was, and you may want to talk to someone who is knowledgeable in this area.

Appendix
Additional Resources

GRIEF

Grieving the Loss of Someone You Love, Raymond R. Mitsch and Lynn Brookside, Vine Books, 1993.

*Tear Soup, book and video, Pat Schwiebert and Chuck DeKlyen.

*When Children Grieve, John James and Russell Friedman, HarperCollins, 2001.

HOLIDAY GRIEF

Journaling Your December Grief, Harold Ivan Smith, Beacon Hill, 2001.

SUDDEN DEATH

No Time for Goodbyes, Janice Harris Lord, Pathfinder Publishing, 1987.

LOSING A CHILD

*Holding On to Hope, Nancy Guthrie, Tyndale, 2002.

LOSING A PARENT

Losing a Parent, Fiona Marshall, Fisher Books, 2000.

Grieving the Death of a Mother, Harold Ivan Smith, Augsburg Press, 2003.

SUICIDE

*Survivors of Suicide, Rita Robinson, New Page, 2001.

Healing after the Suicide of a Loved One, Ann Smolen and John Guinn, A Fireside Book, 1993.

Aftershock, Broadman & Holman Publishers, 2003.

HELPING OTHERS

Helping Those That Hurt, H. Norman Wright, Bethany House, 2003.

The New Guide to Crisis and Trauma Counseling, H. Norman Wright, Regal Books, 2003.

Helping Others Recover from Loss and Grief, curriculum, H. Norman Wright, Christian Marriage Enrichment, 2001.

These books can be ordered from Christian Marriage Enrichment, 800-875-7560.

Notes

CHAPTER 1, "THE FACES OF GRIEF"

1. Gregory Floyd, *In Grief Unveiled* (Brewster, Mass.: Paraclete Press, 1999), 116–17.

2. Ibid.

3. Lilly Singer, Margaret Sirot, and Susan Rodd, *Beyond Loss* (New York: E. P. Dutton, 1988), 62.

4. John Steinbeck, *The Grapes of Wrath* (New York: Penguin Books, 1939), 4–5.

5. Ken Gire, *The Weathering Grace of God* (Ann Arbor, Mich.: Servant Publications, 2001), 90–94.

CHAPTER 2, "PAIN AND DENIAL"

1. Gerald Sittser, *A Grace Disguised* (Grand Rapids, Mich.: Zondervan, 1996), 47.

2. Ibid., 50.

3. Gire, *The Weathering Grace of God,* 69.

CHAPTER 3, "GRIEF IS SO DISRUPTIVE"

1. Raymond R. Mitsch and Lynn Brookside, *Grieving the Loss of Someone You Love* (Ann Arbor, Mich.: Servant Publications, 1993), adapted, 136–38.

2. Kenneth R. Mitchell and Herbert Anderson, *All Our Losses, All Our Griefs* (Philadelphia: Westminster Press, 1983), 92–93.

3. Ibid., 87–93.

4. Anne Morrow-Lindbergh, In *Camp's Unfamiliar Quotations,* 124.

5. Martha Whitmore Hickman, *Healing after Loss* (New York: Perennial, HarperCollins, 1994), 18.

CHAPTER 4, "THE NATURE OF GRIEF"

1. Harold Ivan Smith, *Friendgrief* (Amityville, N.Y.: Baywood Publishing, 2002), 2.

2. Ibid., 9.

3. Therese A. Rando, *Grieving: How to Go On Living When Someone You Love Dies* (Lexington, Mass.: Lexington Books, 1988), 11–12.

CHAPTER 5, "WHY GRIEF?"

1. Rando, *Grieving: How to Go On Living When Someone You Love Dies*, 18–19.

2. As quoted in Bob Diets, *Life after Loss* (Tucson, Ariz.: Fisher Books, 1988), 148.

3. Robert Veninga, *A Gift of Hope* (Boston: Little, Brown and Company, 1985), 71.

CHAPTER 6, "WHAT GRIEF DOES"

1. Ron Mehl, *God Works the Night Shift* (Sisters, Ore.: Multnomah, 1995).

2. Carol Staudacher, *Beyond Grief* (Oakland, Calif.: New Harbinger Publications, 1987), adapted, 47.

3. Mitsch and Brookside, *Grieving the Loss of Someone You Love*, 141–42.

CHAPTER 7, "HOLES IN YOUR LIFE"

1. Phil Rich, *The Healing Journey through Grief* (New York: John Wiley and Sons, 1999), 223–30.

2. Billy Sprague, *A Letter to a Grieving Heart* (Eugene, Ore.: Harvest House, 2001), 9.

3. Arthur Freeze, *Help for Your Grief* (1977), 50.

4. Harry and Cheryl Salem, *From Grief to Glory* (New Kensington, Penn.: Whitaker House, 2003), 89.

CHAPTER 8, "THE QUESTIONS OF GRIEF"

1. Judy Tatelbaum, *The Courage to Grieve* (New York: Perennial, 1980), 28.

2. Gire, *The Weathering Grace of God*, 109.

3. Ibid., 69.

4. Craig Barnes, *When God Interrupts* (Downer's Grove, Ill.: InterVarsity Press, 1996), 135.

5. Rich, *The Healing Journey through Grief*, 90.

CHAPTER 9, "THE EXPRESSION OF TEARS"

1. Nicholas Wolterstoff, *Lament for a Son* (Grand Rapids, Mich.: William B. Eerdman's Publishing Co., 1987), 26.

2. Sprague, *A Letter to a Grieving Heart*, 15.

3. Ibid., 15–16.
4. Mitsch and Brookside, *Grieving the Loss of Someone You Love,* 106.
5. Max Lucado, *No Wonder They Call Him the Savior* (Portland, Ore.: Multnomah Press, 1986), 105–06.
6. Ken Gire, *Windows of the Soul* (Grand Rapids, Mich.: Zondervan, 1996), 195.
7. Ibid., 196.

CHAPTER 10, "NEW UNINVITED GUESTS"
1. Doug Manning, *Don't Take My Grief Away from Me* (San Francisco: Harper, 1979), 41.
2. Floyd, *In Grief Unveiled,* 122–23.

CHAPTER 11, "THE INVASION OF FEAR AND ANXIETY"
1. Therese A. Rando, *Grieving,* 25–29.

CHAPTER 12, "WHAT DO I DO WITH MY GUILT?"
1. Rando, *Grieving,* 32–33.
2. Manning, *Don't Take My Grief Away from Me,* 53–54.
3. Earl A. Grollman, *Living When a Loved One Has Died* (Boston: Beacon Press, 1987), 39–41.

CHAPTER 13, "I'M ANGRY"
1. "Angry at God" excerpt taken from *Under His Wings* by Patsy Claremont (www.healinghouse.org).

CHAPTER 14, "WILL THE SADNESS EVER GO AWAY?"
1. Georgia Shaffer, *A Gift of Mourning Glories* (Ann Arbor, Mich.: Servant Publications, 2000), 28.
2. Nancy Guthrie, *Holding on to Hope* (Wheaton, Ill.: Tyndale House, 2002), 11–12.

CHAPTER 15, "WHAT DO I DO WITH MY FEELINGS?"
1. David W. Willske, *Gone but Not Lost* (Grand Rapids, Mich.: 1992), 55.
2. This experience came from a friend of the author.
3. Grollman, *Living When a Loved One Has Died,* 15–17.

CHAPTER 16, "THE FEELING NO ONE TALKS ABOUT"
1. Jennifer Elison and Chris McGonigle, *Liberating Losses* (Cambridge, Mass.: Perseus Books, Cambridge Center, 2003), 48.

2. Ibid., 73, 106.
3. Ibid., 127–29.
4. Ibid., 153.

CHAPTER 17, "COMPLICATED DEATHS"

1. Tatelbaum, *The Courage to Grieve,* 15.
2. Therese A. Rando, *Treatment of Complicated Mourning* (Champaign, Ill.: Research Press, 1993), 556–57.
3. Helen Fitzgerald, *The Mourning Handbook* (New York: Simon & Schuster, 1994).

CHAPTER 19, "CAPTURING THE MEMORIES"

1. Rich, *The Healing Journey through Grief,* 130–34.

CHAPTER 20, "RECOVERY—IT WILL HAPPEN"

1. Glen W. Davidson, *Understanding Mourning* (Minneapolis: Augsburg Publishing House, 1984), 24–27.
2. Diets, *Life after Loss,* 126–33.
3. Joyce Rupp, *Praying Our Goodbyes* (New York: Ivy Books, 1988), 94–97.

CHAPTER 21, "UNFINISHED ISSUES"

1. Lewis B. Smedes, *Forgive and Forget* (New York: Harper & Row, 1984), 37.

CHAPTER 22, "SAYING GOOD-BYE"

1. Adapted from material developed by Terry Irish, Community Grief Support Group, Crescent City Church of the Nazarene, Crescent City, Calif., and Doctrinal Thesis at Nazarene Theological Seminary, Kansas City, Missouri.
2. Manning, *Don't Take My Grief Away from Me,* 121–22.
3. Rupp, *Praying Our Goodbyes,* 7–8.
4. Ibid., 20–21.
5. James A. Fogarty, *The Magical Thoughts of Grieving Children* (Amityville, N.Y.: Baywood Publishing Co., 2000), 90–91.

CHAPTER 23, "HOW YOUR LIFE WILL CHANGE"

1. Rupp, *Praying Our Goodbyes,* 50–52.
2. Rando, *Grieving,* 280–83.
3. Susan J. Zonnebelt-Smeenge and Robert C. DeVries, *The Empty Chair* (Grand Rapids, Mich.: Baker Book House, 2001), 52.
4. Rando, *Grieving,* 285–86.

CHAPTER 24, "SAYING GOOD-BYE TO GRIEF"

1. Davidson, *Understanding Mourning*, 78–80.

2. Fitzgerald, *The Mourning Handbook*, 249–50.

3. Ann Kaiser Stearns, *Coming Back* (New York: Random House, 1988), 85–86.

4. Claire Cloninger, *Postcards for Those That Hurt* (Dallas: Word Publishing, 1995), 55.

5. Mitsch and Brookside, *Grieving the Loss of Someone You Love*, 177–78.

CHAPTER 25, "TRAUMA—THE DEEPEST WOUND"

1. Robert Hicks, *Failure to Scream* (Nashville, Tenn.: Thomas Nelson, 1993), 46.